THE LEGACY OF
MAIMONIDES

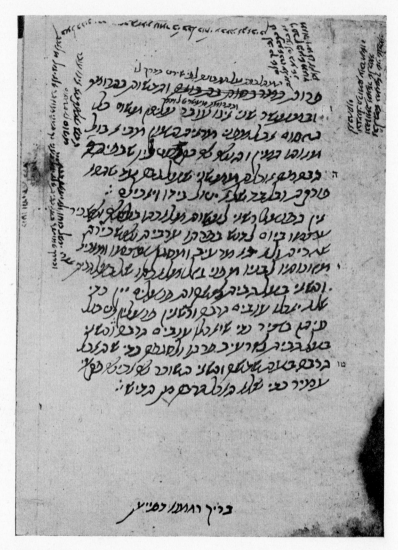

Page of Maimonides' *Mishneh Torah* (Hilkoth Sekiroth chapter XIII 4-7).
Written by the author himself (Autograph). Discovered by M. Lutzki in the
Geniza collection of the Bodleian Library, Oxford, England, and published
by him in the Mishneh Torah edition of Shulsinger Brothers, New York
1947, at end of vol. 5.

THE
LEGACY
OF
MAIMONIDES

by

BEN ZION BOKSER

PHILOSOPHICAL LIBRARY
NEW YORK

Printed in the United States of America.

To Kallia in gratitude.

PREFACE

There have been numerous studies on the life and work of Maimonides, but most of them are in German, a tribute to the culture of the Jewish community in pre-Nazi Germany. The most recent full-length biography of Maimonides in English is that of Solomon Zeitlin, under the title, *Maimonides,* which was published in 1935. It is an exhaustive story of the career of Maimonides, and it includes a detailed characterization of his major writings. Dr. Alexander Marx is the author of a brief biographical sketch of Maimonides which was published in 1935 by the Maimonides Octicentennial Committee as part of a series commemorating the eight-hundredth anniversary of the birth of Maimonides. Despite its brevity, it offers an excellent summation of all that is known about Maimonides as a historical personality. *Maimonides* by D. Yellin and I. Abrahams (Philadelphia, 1903) is a biographical study with special regard to the history of the period in which Maimonides lived.

There is no one book in English interpreting the world outlook of Maimonides, but a fine chapter on Maimonides was included by Isaac Husik in his *History of Medieval Jewish Philosophy.* An anthology of representative selections from the various writings of Maimonides is available in the *Teachings of Maimonides* by A. Cohen, which was published in London in 1927. *The Guide to the Perplexed: Moses Maimonides,* by Leon Roth (London, 1948) offers a fine discussion of a number of problems in the philosophy of Maimonides, and it attempts to place him in the history of thought. It also includes a good biographical sketch of Maimonides, and a bibliography of his numerous writings. There are also two volumes of essays touching on various aspects of the works of Maimonides, one produced in England (London, 1935) under the editorship of I. Epstein, and the other, produced in this country (Columbia University Press, 1941) under the editorship of S. Baron.

PREFACE

The study here presented is an attempt to portray the inner system of ideas which informs the varied writings of Maimonides. It is based primarily on his discussions in the *Guide to the Perplexed,* but his other works were consulted as well. A philosopher remains a philosopher even in his unguarded moments, and relevant philosophical material appears throughout his writings. They were all drawn upon for whatever light they could shed on the Maimonidean world outlook. The biographical sketch with which this study begins is intended only as an introduction, to place Maimonides in the context of the times in which he lived and did his work.

The inception of this study goes back to a series of lectures delivered at the Institute for Religious and Social Studies in the Spring of 1944. The author is indebted to Dr. Louis Ginzberg for a number of suggestions; to Dr. Louis Finkelstein for constant encouragement and inspiration; to Dr. Abraham Joshua Heschel for many helpful discussions of problems in the study of Maimonides; and Dr. Leo Strauss for numerous helpful criticisms and suggestions, which have deepened his understanding of Maimonides and of Jewish philosophy generally. He is also indebted to Dr. Michael Higger and Rabbi Bernard Mandelbaum and to several other friends for technical assistance.

THE LEGACY OF MAIMONIDES

TABLE OF CONTENTS

Chapter I
Introduction
MOSES MAIMONIDES — HIS LIFE AND WORK

Moses ben Maimon was the foremost intellectual figure to arise in medieval Judaism. He was the mediator between two seemingly incompatible world views—the Greek and the rabbinic. Out of ancient Greece there had come the claim of the intellect to sole competence in leading a man to the truth about himself and about the world. Not faith, not a revealed Scripture, not a divine law, but reason operating in the cold syllogisms of logical demonstration was to be a man's guide toward the wisdom he needs for his life. All this was negated by the world view of rabbinic Judaism which warned man that reason was but a frail reed to lean on, that only in the divinely revealed Scripture was he to find a dependable truth, and that by conformity to the divine law alone would he find true happiness. The gulf between these two outlooks was wide indeed—and seemingly impassable. Maimonides had mastered both doctrines, but beyond their conflicts he saw the common ground of a higher synthesis. His synthesis constitutes one of the most important chapters in the history of human thought and represents a significant contribution toward man's understanding of the world and of his destiny within it.

Maimonides was a man of great erudition and rare versatility. He wrote with remarkable power on astronomy, medicine, logic, liturgy, philosophy and jurisprudence. He wrote commentaries on the Mishnah and the Talmud. He composed a code of Jewish law which offers brilliant systemization of a highly heterogeneous and complex mass of material. He wrote occasional essays dealing with the cogent problems of his time. He carried on an extensive correspondence with people all over the world who consulted him on various problems in philosophy and religion as well as in practical affairs.

1

All this he accomplished amidst a busy and active life, beset by fierce distractions. He was born on March 30, 1135, in Cordova, Spain. When he was thirteen years of age he joined his family in flight before the invading Almohades who brought with them religious intolerance, inaugurating a policy of persecution for non-Moslems. For twelve years the Maimon family was without a fixed home. They settled in Fez, North Africa, but were forced to pose as Moslems. After five years of a "Marrano" existence, Moses sailed for Palestine, in the hope that there he might find freedom. But the Palestine of that day proved uninviting. The Moslem-Christian wars for the Holy Land had left the country in ruins. The small Jewish community of no more than a thousand souls was poor. Their culture was decadent. Another hope proved illusory, and once more he was forced to wander.

Maimonides finally settled in Cairo, Egypt. Trouble, however, then came to him from a new direction. Maimonides had been a partner in his brother's jewelry business, which gave him an ample income without imposing heavy obligations on him. But now his brother died in a shipwreck in the Indian Ocean while on one of his business trips, and with him went down the entire family fortune. Thus Maimonides was now confronted with the problem of a livelihood. He could not support his family as a professional rabbi. The rabbinate in those days was not a profession. The rabbi usually earned his living by means of some other gainful occupation, without accepting any remuneration for the performance of his religious duties.

Fortunately, Maimonides had studied medicine, and he now became a practicing physician. His fame as a physician spread rapidly. In time he became the court physician to the Sultan Saladin, and afterward to Saladin's son, Al-Afdhal. He also became the official head of the Cairo Jewish community. Even in Cairo, however, his life was not one of leisure, and he could not give himself uninterruptedly to literary activity. His duties as a physician were heavy and exacting, and his responsibilities as the leader of Cairo Jewry were heavy as well.

An often quoted letter to his friend and translator Judah ibn Tibbon, offers us a glimpse into his busy and burdened life. "My duties to the Sultan are very heavy," he writes. "I am obliged to visit him every day, early in the morning, and when he or any of his children, or any of the inmates of his harem, are indisposed, I dare not quit Cairo, but must stay during the greater part of the day in the palace. It also frequently happens that one or two of the royal officers fall sick, and I must attend to their healing. Hence, as a rule, I repair to Kahira very early in the day, and even if nothing unusual happens, I do not return to Forstat (his home, about 1½ miles away) until the afternoon. Then I am almost dying with hunger. I find the ante-chambers filled with people, both Jews and Gentiles, nobles and common people, judges and bailiffs, friends and foes—a mixed multitude, who await the time of my return.

"I dismount from my animal, wash my hands, go forth to my patients, and entreat them to bear with me while I partake of some slight refreshments, the only meal I take in the twenty-four hours. Then I attend to my patients, and write prescriptions and directions for their several ailments. Patients go in and out until nightfall, and sometimes, even, I solemnly assure you, until two hours and more into the night. I converse and prescribe for them while lying down from sheer fatigue, and when night falls I am so exhausted that I can scarcely speak.

"Thus no Israelite can have a private interview with me except on the Sabbath. On that day the whole Congregation, or at least the majority of the members, come to me after the morning service, when I instruct (advise) them as to their proceedings during the whole week; we study together a little until noon, when they depart. Some of them return, and read with me after the afternoon service until evening prayers. In this manner I spend that day."[1]

His duties as court physician proved burdensome, however, not merely because of the time they consumed. He had to face political intrigue, and to steer himself subtly against the pitfalls of those serving in high places. Especially as a Jew he found his position often precarious. We have an echo of his difficulties in one of his letters which has come down to us:

"The high offices to which Jews attain these days are not to me an unmitigated good-fortune worthy to strive after. As the Lord liveth, they are actually evils of no small proportions. For the perfect man who enjoys true bliss is one who attends to the perfection of the religious life and the performance of his obligations, and who shuns all the evils of men and all ugly human traits. But the person who holds public office is subject to many distresses, for he may lose favor with the gentiles and be degraded by them, and he may fall into the power of the state and suffer harsh treatment and bodily harm. And if, on the other hand, he always bends his ways to conform to the desires of the people, he will have placed himself against the Torah of the Lord, becoming a sycophant and a flatterer."[2]

The Writings of Maimonides

Maimonides began his literary career at an early age. His earliest work, written at the age of sixteen, was the *Millot ha-Higayon.* It is a succinct exposition of the meaning of various technical terms in logic and metaphysics. It was written in Arabic, and then translated into Hebrew. Its Hebrew version helped standardize a philosophical vocabulary for the Hebrew language which was followed by later writers on the subject. Another of his early works was his *Essay on the Calendar,* written originally in Arabic, but now available only in Hebrew translation. It is a penetrating study of a complicated subject, and reveals his fine powers as a mathematician.

The first great work of Maimonides was the commentary on the Mishnah which he began at the age of 23 and completed in ten years. The Mishnah, summarizing the opinions of the great masters of Jewish law who functioned in the Palestinian academies until the third century of the common era, had come down as a brief and highly concise document. The Babylonian and Palestinian Talmuds were based on it, and to that extent offered some exposition of it. But the teachers of the Talmud were concerned with the formulation of law, and with the use of the Mishnah as a source book of law; they were not concerned with interpreting the Mishnah text as such. It was this important task which Maimonides performed for students of the Mishnah.

His commentary is concerned with elucidating the individual passage as well as the larger theme to which it is addressed. He defines words and phrases, entering upon philological discussions when necessary. He supplies archeological and scientific background to certain texts without which they cannot be made intelligible. He prefaces some parts of the Mishnah with introductory statements, and wherever ethical or theological questions are raised, he enters upon a full analysis of the subject, bringing to bear upon these themes all his powers as a philosopher.

Some of these introductions and philosophical discussions have become famous in themselves, without reference to the text on which they are based. These include the historical introduction to the Mishnah, with which the work begins; the famous eight chapters on psychology which appear in his discussions on the ethical treatise *Abot;* and the creed of thirteen articles summarizing the teachings of his faith, which is offered in the course of his comments on the tenth chapter of *Sanhedrin,* in the introduction to *Helek.* The creed includes the belief in the existence of God, His unity, non-corporeality, and eternity; that man can and should enter into worshipful communion with Him; that He inspires man with prophetic illumination; the primacy of Moses among the prophets; the divine origin of the Torah; that the Torah will not be abrogated in favor of any new dispensation; divine providence; retribution; the Messianic redemption; and life after death. The creed was never formally adopted in Judaism, but its popularity and influence is attested by the fact that it was included in all standard editions of the Jewish prayerbook and recommended for recitation at the conclusion of each morning service.

The ten years during which he labored on the commentary coincided with his wanderings while in flight from Spain, and it is a tribute to the consecration with which he worked that persecutions and exile did not deflect him from his task. He alludes to the circumstances under which he wrote in a concluding note to this work: "If there be one who shall discover an inaccuracy in this commentary, or shall have a better explanation to offer, let my attention be directed to it; and let me be exonerated by the fact that I have worked with far greater application than any one who writes for the sake of pay or profit, and that I have worked under the most trying circumstances. For Heaven hath ordained that we be exiled and we were therefore driven about from place to place; I was thus impelled to work on the commentary while traveling by land or crossing the sea. I, Moses ben Maimon commenced it when I was twenty-three years old and finished it in Egypt at the age of thirty-three years . . ."

The commentary was originally written in Arabic. In its Hebrew translation it has been included in every standard edition of the Talmud and the Mishnah. It has remained an invaluable interpretation of the Mishnah text, surpassed by none preceding or following it.

Maimonides spent another ten years in the compilation of what is the great classic of Jewish law, the *Mishneh Torah,* the Torah Reviewed, or the *Yad ha-Hazakah,* the Mighty Hand (*Yad,* hand, has in Hebrew the numerical value of 14, the number of books in the code). It is a digest of the entire range of Jewish law, and Maimonides composed it in a fine, classical Hebrew. The *Mishneh Torah* is a triumph of the art of systematization. It brings together the entire body of Talmudic law and doctrine in all its vastness, all its diversity into one coherent whole, rendering final decisions as a guide to action. Each of the fourteen books into which the code is divided deals with a number of commandments that comprise a general theme. The first two books offer an outline of his teachings in theology and ethics. More than 200 commentaries have been written on the Mishneh Torah, testifying to its popularity and to the earnestness with which it was studied in later generations.

In his *Mishneh Torah* Maimonides arranged the Biblical commandments in a new order rejecting the arrangement originally established by Rabbi Simon Kahira. Maimonides believed that the order established by Rabbi Simon was inaccurate and he felt called on to challenge it, despite its popularity. But Maimonides was concerned lest he be criticized by the unsophisticated, tradition-bound populace for breaking with older authorities. As Maimonides put it: "And when I considered and realized the popularity of the conventional arrangement (of the commandments) among the common people, I knew that if I should mention the true arrangement . . . the first reader will resolve in his mind that it is in error. And the evidence of error will be for him its deviation from what so-and-so stated. For, this is the feeling among the 'educated' men in our time, and surely among the multitude—they do not examine a statement by its contents, but by its conformity to the statement of a previous author, without having evaluated the former statement" (Introduction, the *Book of Precepts*).

As a result of these apprehensions, Maimonides wrote the *Book of Precepts*. It is a kind of introduction to the *Mishneh Torah,* justifying the method of its arrangement and the order in which the commandments are organized. It is written in Arabic, and presented in a popular style, designed especially to reach the less sophisticated reader. In later years Maimonides regretted that he had not written it in Hebrew. While intended primarily to deal with anticipated criticisms of the *Mishneh Torah,* it was acclaimed widely for its fine discussions on the nature and functions of law, and for its many fine insights into the commandments of the Bible.

The most imposing philosophical work of Maimonides was the *Moreh Nebuchim,* or the *Guide to the Perplexed.* He began working on it about the year 1185, and sent installments of it, as he finished them, to his pupil Joseph ibn Aknin, to whom the entire work is dedicated. He labored on it for approximately fifteen years.[3] It is the greatest philosophic work produced in Judaism. Its aim is to meet the challenge of Greek philosophy, especially that of Aristotle's naturalism, to the doctrines and practices of his traditional religion. Maimonides wrote this great work in Arabic, but it has been translated into most modern languages. The *Moreh* is organized around the teachings of the Bible which required clarification or justification, rather than the logical order of doctrines in philosophy. Its ideas became the basis for all subsequent writings in Jewish philosophy, and even the Cabbalists and the mystics who reacted against its rationalism, drew much of their inspiration from it.

The influence of the *Moreh* extended beyond the Jewish community. It influenced the great writers of scholasticism, Alexander of Hales, Albertus Magnus, John Scotus, and especially Thomas Aquinas. Moslem theologians were influenced by it as well. Even modernists like Spinoza and Leibniz, despite their criticism of it in details, found in this work of Maimonides a source book for some of their ideas and a precedent for their own intellectual labors.

Maimonides was also the author of a number of minor works. The most important of these are the *Letter on Apostasy,* the *Epistle to Yemen,* the *Letter on Astrology,* the *Essay on the Resurrection of the Dead,* and a large volume of Responsa. Most of this material deals with problems facing various Jewish communities who had turned to Maimonides for advice and guidance.[4]

The minor works of Maimonides also include a number dealing with various aspects of Jewish law. There are references to his commentaries on several tractates of the Talmud but not much is known of them. His commentary on *Rosh Hashanah* has been published but there is some doubt as to its authenticity. Of his commentary on *Shabbat* only fragments remain.[5] And only recently has his legal digest based on the Palestine Talmud been discovered. Portions of this work were published in Dr. Louis Ginzberg's *Jerushalmi Fragments from the Genizah,* which was issued by the Jewish Theological Seminary in 1909. In those days, however, the author of those fragments could not be identified. The identification has since been made, and a new creation of Maimonides has become known to us. Dr. Saul Lieberman offers us an exhaustive study of this work, the cogent elements which identify it as that of Maimonides, and its relation to other Maimonidean writings, in an anotated edition under the title *Hilkot ha-Yerushalmi* (the Laws of the Palestine Talmud). It was issued by the Jewish Theological Seminary in 1947.

The contributions of Maimonides to medicine are less well-known but they were significant. Maimonides wrote at least ten works on medicine. His *Aphorisms,* consisting of twenty-four chapters, was his most popular work on medicine. It deals with anatomy, physiology, pathology, gynecology, personal hygiene, gymnastics and physical training. Another popular work was a miscellany of health rules, dedicated to the Sultan al-Afdhal. In this book he stressed the importance of moderate living for proper health. His book on hemorrhoids suggested what foods those afflicted must especially avoid, and he recommended various drugs by which to cure the disease. He also wrote on asthma, sex, and reptile poisons and their antidotes.[6]

These works were all written in Arabic, but some were later translated into Hebrew and German. As to the scientific value of these works, one medical critic recently characterized them thus:— "Maimonides' medical teachings are not antiquated at all. His writings, in fact, are in some respects astonishingly modern in tone and contents."[7] The detailed appraisal of the well-known medical historian Max Neuberger is more specific: "In his medical works Maimonides shows himself an erudite and experienced physician, wholly free from mysticism, a soberly-observant clinician who displayed in his therapeutics a decided preference for dietetic and expectant modes of treatment. In matters of theory he remained faithful to Galenism, but his intimate knowledge of its doctrines led him upon occasion to criticize the Pergumene."[8]

The Controversy About Maimonides

Maimonides won for himself a great host of friends and admirers, who recognized at once this great genius as a scholar and philosopher, and as the architect of the most formidable intellectual defense of Judaism. It was natural, however, that his writings should also evoke opposition from those unaccustomed to such boldness and originality in thinking. There were objections to his code because he included therein some of his advanced ideas in theology, and because, in an effort to achieve greater lucidity, he had omitted the citation of sources. The very popularity of the code alarmed some lest it displace the Talmud as the principal subject of rabbinic study. Some critics were simply unable to follow the reasoning behind his conclusions. His principal philosophical work, the *Guide to the Perplexed,* was criticized because it seemed like a work of unblushing rationalism, taking its cues from Aristotle, rather than from the time-honored teachings of tradition.

There were arguments and counter-arguments. Maimonides was anxious to avoid public controversy, and he sought to minimize his departure from conventional ideas. This is why he placed many of his ideas, especially in the *Guide,* in veiled language, frequently hinting at his thoughts, rather than expressing them fully. He wrote his treatise on the Resurrection to defend his orthodoxy, to refute the charge that he disbelieved in a bodily resurrection in the hereafter. We have noted previously that he wrote *The Book of Precepts* to justify his arrangement of the commandments in the *Mishneh Torah,* where he rejected the customary order which had been initiated by Rabbi Simon Kahira.

Maimonides never claimed infallibility. "I never pride myself of not making mistakes," he wrote on one occasion. "On the contrary, when I discover one, or if I am convinced of an error by others, I am ready to change anything in my writings, in my ways and even in my nature." At the same time, when convinced he was right, he knew how to maintain his position without faltering. He was fully aware that in the final analysis a man's business is to please God and not man, and that truth ranked higher than the consent of the multitude. As he put it in the introduction to the *Guide*: "When I find the road narrow and can see no other way of teaching a well-established truth except by pleasing one intelligent man and displeasing ten thousand fools— I prefer to address myself to the one man and take no notice whatever of the condemnation of the multitude."

Some of the opposition to Maimonides developed in his own life-time, but Maimonides ignored his opponents. He was content to have his works speak for themselves, and to leave the final judgment to the verdict of history. As he wrote to his pupil, ibn Aknin: "Even when men insult me, I do not mind, but answer kindly with friendly words or remain silent. . . . I shall never fight on my own behalf, for my dignity and the honor of my character are too dear to me to engage in a war of words with the ignorant." He pleaded with his pupils, who were eager to defend their master's honor, to do likewise . . . to shun disputations and to ignore the calumny of his enemies. "All the better," he wrote to an admirer, Joseph ibn Gabar, about one of his opponents, "if he hopes to gain credit by his conduct. He may win and I shall certainly not lose."

Maimonides knew human folly too well to be shocked that there were men who rejected what his genius had brought them for their own enlightenment. "Not to appreciate the value of this book" (the Code), he expounded in a plea to a disciple, "is no worse than not knowing various principles of metaphysics of which they are ignorant. If a person should become upset and bitter because of every one who is ignorant of a particular truth or who denies stubbornly matters on which there is no doubt, or who maintains devotedly a certain perverse idea, he is bound to spend all his days in grief. . . . It is not proper to behave thus."

One cannot fight such folly directly, by polemicizing against it. One can only proclaim the truth, and those who are ready for it will welcome it ardently. And that was the course he recommended. "God willing," Maimonides continued to plead, "If you should teach . . . those who are qualified to understand and set forth the beauty of this work and disseminate it among people, it will be more pleasing both to you and to me than the polemics."

As Maimonides reached old age, a touch of disillusionment came over him. The world yielded itself but slowly to ideal influences. He found comfort in his studies and in his gifted son, Abraham. In a fragment of a note which has come down to us, he writes: "When I consider the condition of the world, I find consolation in only these two . . . contemplating and studying whatever I study, and in my son, Abraham. . . . He is the essence of modesty and also a man of noble character traits, of a keen mind and excellent talent. . . . I pray that the Lord may watch over him and shower upon him His fullest bounty."[9]

Maimonides died in 1204, at the age of sixty-nine. It was after his death that the opposition to his work took on a really violent character. There were even excommunications and counter-excommunications. In 1233, one zealot, Rabbi Solomon of Montpelier, succeeded in inducing the church authorities to add the *Guide* to the list of heretical books, which the church was then trying to eliminate from circulation, and this great masterpiece of Jewish thought was consigned to the flames. As many copies as could be collected were burnt in a great bonfire, lit by a torch furnished by the altar of a Parisian church.

The controversy faded after a time. It is the lot of every pioneer in thought that the world's first reaction is to ignore him, then to vilify him, and finally to acclaim him. Maimonides was too great a man to be ignored. His vilification was intense, but only from a small number and for a short time. Increasingly, as his towering genius made itself felt in the diverse fields of scholarship and thought to which he contributed, he has been acclaimed as one of the greatest and noblest spirits that ever appeared in history.

Chapter II

REASON AND THE QUEST FOR TRUTH

The problem which stirred Maimonides to undertake his philosophical labors was one of the perennial problems in human thought—the conflict between religion and scientific naturalism. Still in the early stages of its growth, ancient science had nevertheless reached a high degree of sophistication in its philosophical discussions. In Aristotle it found a spokesman who was able to pose a challenge with which religious thinkers are still grappling in our own time. Of all those immense secrets which modern scientists have been wresting from the unknown, Aristotle knew little. A college freshman has at his command a more imposing body of facts concerning the nature of existence than did that mightiest intellect of ancient Greece. But Aristotle had an intuition which remains at the heart of the boldest interpreters of science in our day. He started from the proposition that the way to truth is reason. By the operations of the intellect alone, man was to seek and find whatever truth he needed about the world. The intellect alone was to help us find an outlook on the universe no less than a code of moral conduct by which to live in it.

Aristotle was no atheist. His metaphysics was rather polite to many religious conceptions. He affirmed the existence of a God who was the beginning and the end of all existence. The universe he portrayed had order and beauty. Human beings were given a challenge worthy of their best efforts—to strive for perfection. But those religious affirmations of an Aristotelian philosophy had little in common with traditional religion. God, in the metaphysical system of Aristotle, is the unmoved mover, the absolute mind whose sole activity is eternal self-contemplation. He generates activity and motion in all things, because being perfect, He excites in all other beings a longing to become like Him, to imitate His perfection. But He cannot act freely to initiate purposes of His choosing. Like all other beings in nature, He is a prisoner in an all-inclusive system of determinism, held in check by its laws, and limited by its actions and their consequences.

The philosophy of Aristotle, like every naturalism down to our own time, is in fundamental opposition to the basic claims of traditional religion. The insistence that reason alone offers us truth undermines the basis of a revealed Scripture, and of the belief in the special vocation of any particular religious community. A God who is incapable of free decision and free initiative and whose actions must always conform to natural law cannot of course perform miracles. He cannot respond to prayer. What is perhaps even more serious, such a God can concern Himself only with a general order of nature, but hardly with individual members of the species. In traditional religion the individual person is looked upon as a center of supreme value, the object of God's special solicitude. A "naturalistic" religion may help a philosopher explain the universe, but it offers us very little of the things which can help us live in it. For the universe it portrays is cold and soulless and indifferent to man and to the deepest yearnings of his nature.

The crux of the controversy between naturalism and traditional religion centered on whether the universe was to be regarded as created or eternal. The naturalists in maintaining the impossibility of creation in time were simply following the logic of their doctrine that natural necessity is the sole factor in determining events. Creation out of nothing is a complete contradiction of natural causality. When there was nothing, there was no nature and there was no cause at work to bring about what had not existed before. The belief in a created universe was the total rejection of natural determinism, and it implied the belief that God could act freely to pursue whatever purposes seemed good to Him.[1]

The adherents of traditional religion sensed keenly the peril in these doctrines advanced in the name of Aristotle. Some therefore turned hostile to philosophy. Enough for a man to study

Scripture, to master God's word, and to live by His holy law. The speculative studies were a peril to man's soul. They would alienate him from his traditional moorings, and make him a heretic, a disbeliever.

There were others who pretended to "reconcile" religion and philosophy. They elaborated theories which never came to grips with the underlying issues in the challenge of Aristotelian natural-ism. All they cared for was to answer Aristotle, and whatever seemed to answer him, they accepted as true, whether or not it would stand up under critical analysis. The principal goal of these men was to prove the creation of the universe, but Mai-monides saw through their "proofs," for, as Maimonides saw it, on purely rational grounds it was impossible to demonstrate crea-tion. This labor of reconciliation was represented in the current religious apologetics of the three religious communities, the Chris-tians, the Moslems and the Jews. As Maimonides characterized these men, they began by examining "what must be the properties of the things which should yield proof for or against a certain creed; when this was ascertained they asserted that the thing must be endowed with those properties." They reasoned in a circle, but at least if one did not think too deeply—they had built a defense for their religious faith.[2]

The issue called for a bolder answer. The timid might be inti-mated by the cry of heresy. The superficial might be contented by the rationalizations of the current apologetics for religion. But those who were intellectually honest, those brave spirits who had eaten of the tree of knowledge and felt its disturbing impact, were confronted by a great dilemma. Their hearts clung to the old faith, while their minds clung to the new doctrine. They were be-wildered, perplexed.

Maimonides addressed himself to these people when he wrote his *Guide to the Perplexed.* As he expressed it in the introduction to this book: "The object of this treatise is to enlighten a religious man who has been trained to believe in our holy law . . . and at the same time has been successful in his philosophical studies.

Human reason has attracted him to abide in its sphere and he finds it difficult to accept as correct the teachings based on the literal interpretations of the law . . . Hence, he is lost in perplexity and anxiety."[3]

Was there an honest answer to the seeming clash between reason and religion? Did reason, pursued to its essential demands, necessarily lead to philosophic naturalism? And did religion really stand for the rejection of the rational examination of existence, for the denial of reason's right to speak on what we are to believe concerning the truth about the universe and man's life in it? Moses ben Maimon denied that such a clash existed. It was possible to find an accommodation, one that would not sacrifice the legitimate rights of the one or the other. A man who has looked deeper into things, who has boldly pursued this controversy in all its ramifications should in the end be able to find peace. The life of reason and the pious devotion to the truths of revealed religion are not incompatible loyalties. They are on the contrary complementary channels through which we are to seek truth. That peace was one of the discoveries of Moses ben Maimon; and it is one of his principal legacies to posterity.

Reason's Road to Truth

Maimonides summoned men to the untrammeled pursuit of the life of reason. The mind is man's distinguishing attribute in the hierarchy of existence. It is a necessary condition of his humanity. The intellectual faculty is what "differentiates the human species and distinguishes it from other species." Without his intellectual powers and the precious fruit of knowledge and doctrine they fashion for him, man sinks to the order of existence below him, the animal. "Before he develops understanding and acquires knowledge," Maimonides declared, "man is accounted as the beast. He is only distinguished from the rest of the animal creation by the consciousness that he is a living being possessed of intellect." To function as a true human being one must therefore seek knowledge through the full pursuit of reason.[4]

The very circumstances of man's physical life call for the application of reason. An animal can live by instinct, for an animal is generally self-sufficient. A man can not live by instinct. The complexity of human existence demands social organization and the specialization of functions among different individuals. All this depends on planning and thinking. "An animal does not require for its sustenance any plan, for all things to which it has to attend it performs by itself. With man it is different . . . For the food which man requires for his subsistence demands much work and preparation, which can only be accomplished by reflection and by plan; many vessels must be used, and many individuals must be employed, each in his own specialized work . . . The protection from heat in summer and from cold in winter, and shelter from rain, snow and wind, require in the same manner the preparation of many things, none of which can properly be done without design and thought. Consequently, if a man were deprived of his intellectual faculties, and possessed only vitality, he would in a short time be lost."

That is the immediate function of the intellect—to aid us in practical affairs, to fashion tools for the service of various human needs. It is responsible for the development of such arts as agriculture, architecture, medicine and navigation. It is also responsible for the rules and regulations governing a social order, for the administration of personal affairs, no less than the affairs of the nation, and the larger community of nations.

The highest expression of reason is theoretic. It is the quest for truth as represented in the general sciences. It is the critical examination of objects and events with a view of distinguishing between appearances and realities, and thus to achieve a body of valid knowledge concerning the nature of things. Reason "analyzes and divides the component parts of things. It forms abstract ideas of them, represents them in their true form as well as in their causal relations, derives from one object a great many facts. It distinguishes that which is the property of the genus from that which is peculiar to the individual . . . The intellect further determines whether certain qualities of things are essential or non-essential."

In this act of analysis and generalization, the intellect functions as what we may call speculative reason. Its goal is to reveal things "as they really are, and which by nature are not subject to change." It frees our knowledge from the casual appearances that objects assume in the flux of existence, reaching down to the unchanging essence that persists amidst all the change.[4]

Some of the most baffling problems in metaphysics can be resolved by the aid of reason. The existence of God, His unity and incorporeality, and various other related doctrines, can be established by the process of reason. And by the aid of reason we can discover the nature and function of the many varied beings that exist in the world. To be sure, the utility of some objects is not clear, simply because science had not yet completed its search for truth. Each generation, as it grows in knowledge, continues to narrow the realm of the unknown and to extend man's awareness of the facts about the world which is his home.[5]

The highest good of human life which is also the principal concern of religion—the love of God—is likewise achieved by way of the intellect. It is the contemplation of nature that yields us knowledge concerning God, concerning His wisdom and beneficence. And that knowledge when it is deep enough develops finally into an emotional response, which is love. Maimonides described the transition from the knowledge to the love of God in these terms: "At the time when one reflects on His works, and His wonderful and stupendous creations, and from them perceives His wisdom which is incomparable and unbounded, he immediately loves, praises, glorifies and yearns with an ardent longing to know the great God . . . And when one reflects upon these very things, he immediately starts back, is struck with fear and terror, and is conscious that he is a creature, insignificant, lowly and immature, standing with only slight and scanty knowledge. As David said (Ps. 8:4-5): 'When I consider Thy heavens, the work of Thy fingers, what is man that Thou art mindful of Him?' "

The climax of man's attitude toward God is emotional; it is love and awe. But the road which leads to it is reason; and no other road is available. For love cannot be assumed at will; it comes as a by-product to comprehension. "One does not love God except through the knowledge that one has of Him, and to the measure of our knowledge will be our love; if little, it will be little, and if much, it will be much."

The pursuit of reason is for Maimonides not only permissible, but mandatory. It is man's duty to pursue the life of reason. Maimonides made the study of philosophy a religious obligation, including it within the command to love God. Since such love hinges upon knowledge, we must seek knowledge as the prelude to love. The command to love God, then, includes all the preliminary steps by which it may be attained; it includes the call "to contemplate His commandments, and His utterances, and His works till we comprehend Him and feel utmost delight in our comprehension of Him, and this is the love concerning which we are obligated."

The act of reason, and the fruit of its labors, science and philosophy, thus steer a man toward the very noblest goals of his life. No wonder Maimonides had a profound reverence for the great spokesman of philosophy, especially for Aristotle. He ranked Aristotle as second only to the prophets. For had not Aristotle carried reason to her supreme triumphs, shedding light on all man's dilemmas about himself, about nature, and about God?[6]

The Insufficiency of Reason

The appreciation of Maimonides for the role of reason in life was profound. But as he continued to reflect on the necessities of human life, he saw clearly enough that reason was not sufficient. In itself it could not be depended on to guide people toward the truth they need for their lives. Most people could not possibly pursue the entire course of reason in order to attain the vital body of doctrine that is to furnish them with the truths they need for their beliefs and their actions. For the way of a philosopher is hard, and many are the pitfalls which will keep a man from attaining its goals.

The study of metaphysics, which seeks the truth concerning God and the universe cannot be a popular occupation. It requires a highly elaborate preliminary education. The novice cannot enter at once into the study of metaphysical problems, which are subtle and difficult. The inquiries into those abstruse problems come at the apex of an educational pyramid. Before entering upon metaphysics one must acquire a knowledge of logic, mathematics, and the natural sciences. One cannot speculate concerning the ultimate character of the universe, without a knowledge of sciences like astronomy and physics, which probe into the nature of things within the universe. And one cannot enter upon such speculations without a due knowledge of the process of reason itself, which is conveyed in logic and mathematics. For many are the pitfalls to successful reasoning. Many are the chances of error. The imagination confuses us with false notions, which have every semblance of truth. The accidental appearances of things under the force of some special circumstances present themselves as though they were essential qualities. Habit pulls us to think along conventional lines, to hold on to accustomed opinions, and to shun innovations. Delusions may be many, while the truth is but one, and to attain truth, one must be able to reason with accuracy and care, to proceed patiently and with the correct premises on which the edifice of our knowledge must be built.

Long and weary is the road by which we must travel toward reason's highest destination. The average man cannot make such a journey. Some men are tempermentally unsuited for it. Patience, calmness, detachment, the ability to adjust to new ideas, emancipation from worldly passions—these are the virtues with which one must be equipped to be a good metaphysician. And how many are fortunate with such endowments? Training, in itself, cannot give us such virtues, which depend in large measure on certain bodily traits and on a certain maturity which comes with the years. People who are excitable, rash or passionate, cannot pursue the goals of philosophy. Young people generally make poor students of metaphysics. They are impeded "on account of the heat of the blood and the flame of youth, which confuses their minds. That heat which causes all disorder must first disappear. They must have become moderate and settled, humble in their hearts, and subdued in their temperaments."

The common man's quest for wisdom is also hindered by his many mundane interests. For man is not a disembodied intelligence; he lives in the world and is subject to its distractions. The need of earning a livelihood for himself and his family will often absorb all his energies and leave him little opportunity for the pursuits of truth. The pressures of the world, moreover, work their subtle influences and we seek not only the necessities of a livelihood but all kinds of luxuries. Then we have neither time nor the inclination to study. "Man is disturbed in his intellectual occupation by the necessity of looking after the material wants of the body, especially if the necessity of providing for wife and children be super-added; much more so if he seeks superfluities in addition to his ordinary wants, for by custom and bad habit these become a powerful motive. Even the perfect man to whom we have referred, if too busy with these necessary things—much more so if busy with unnecessary things, and filled with a great desire for them—must weaken or altogether lose his desire for study, to which he will apply himself with interruption, lassitude and want of attention. He will not attain that for which he is fitted by his abilities, or he will acquire imperfect knowledge, a confused mass of true and false ideas."

Reason would thus be a very inadequate guide for most men in their quest for truth. It is necessarily the domain of a chosen few. If we had to depend on our own reason to establish every article of our belief, most men would die in total ignorance. They would close their years long before discovering "whether there was a God or not, much less that certain things must be asserted about Him, and other things denied as defects."[7]

The philosopher would fare no better if he had to live solely by philosophy. There are many vital areas of life where we need guidance and where man made philosophy cannot help us. For reason has its limits beyond which it does not function effectively.

The most crucial problem in philosophy, whether the universe was eternal or created in time, could not be answered decisively by the considerations of reason. Maimonides denounced those who sought a cheap reconciliation between reason and religion by "proving" creation. But it was just as evident to him that reason could not demonstrate the theory of the eternalists either. Reason is limited to the empirical world, and it cannot speak on questions that take us beyond it. "Therefore, when the mind endeavors to contemplate what is beyond, it is unable to do so for the reason that the matter is too high for it." Here was the most critical doctrine of the naturalists, the principal source of their attacks on traditional religion, and they could not marshal conclusive rational support for their view.[8]

Reason in itself, moreover, cannot create a sound moral code and help us build a just society. And a man is a citizen of the world even when he is a philosopher.

The creation of justice in the world depends on two conditions. It depends on the formulation of a body of legislation by which to define and to enforce the mutual obligations of the citizens of a community. And it involves, on the part of the citizens, the cultivation of personal virtues which will aid them in self-restraint and in bending their private inclinations toward the common good. Where men are motivated by selfish drives, we shall be unable to create a good society. For when men "follow entirely the guidance of lust there is an increase of envy, hatred and warfare for the purpose of taking what another possesses."

But how can we accomplish all this? How can we bring life under moral discipline and create a suitable body of laws that will give us a just society? We cannot do so with reason alone. The definition of good and evil cannot be accomplished on purely theoretical grounds. At most reason can suggest that a certain moral idea is plausible; it cannot affirm it with certainty. The

Aristotelian doctrine of the mean, defining the good as the middle point between two extremes, which had ample parallels in rabbinic literature, and to which Maimonides adhered, offered valuable ethical insights, but it cannot supply guidance for the vast majority of men. For people cannot always tell precisely where lies the middle point of behaviour between the extremes which are to be avoided. And what is to motivate people in the necessary self-discipline which is involved in choosing what is good and renouncing what is evil? Indeed, if we had no other foundations for our moral ideas than those which reason could suggest, we should have to take our notion of what is right from the prevailing opinions of mankind. Morality would thus be reduced to a convention, as uncertain as the shifting winds of popular taste. On such foundations one could not create a stable world justice.[9]

These limitations of reason do not distract from the glories of its achievement, where it is competent to act. But it is clear that man needs something else, in addition to reason, to guide his life. That something else, Maimonides was due to demonstrate, is divine revelation.

Chapter III

HOW SHALL WE THINK OF GOD?

The doctrine which offered the greatest difficulty to thinking men in the time of Maimonides was the belief in God. It was important to prove the existence of God, but it was just as important to take a stand on how we were to think of Him.

We have already called attention to the divergence between traditional religion and the teachings of philosophy on how we were to think of God. Traditional religion conceived God in more or less human terms. He was spoken of as a person, endowed with physical organs and subject to emotional states. The philosophers looked upon such a conception of God as naive and as unworthy of a thinking man. The God they believed in was an impersonal force, without free will and without the capacity to alter the course of the universe which proceeded in accordance with the laws of natural necessity. Maimonides examined carefully the conflict between tradition and philosophy and he elaborated a doctrine which offers effective mediation between them.

Proving the Existence of God

Two proofs for the existence of God were current in educated circles at the time of Maimonides. The dominant school of Moslem theology, also followed by many Christians and Jews, proved the existence of God from the doctrine of a created universe. The universe, it was argued, is clearly a composite, formed from certain ultimate pre-existent elements. But these very "ultimate pre-existent elements" must have had a "cause." A created universe necessarily implied a creator. The advantage of this proof was that it at once disposed of all limitations in God's activity. A universe fashioned out of nothing cannot place limitations in the path of its creator. He is above it, and wholly sov-

24

ereign over it. This proof was therefore popular among those eager to defend traditional religion.

Maimonides refused to accept this proof because in some re-spect it begged the question. It was based on the doctrine of crea-tion, but this very doctrine was disputed by the Aristotelians. There were arguments for creation but they were not conclusive; and some men were not convinced by them. The heart of all religious faith—the belief in the existence of God—should not be based on proofs that were subject to challenge. If we want to prove the existence of God, then we must work with the assump-tions of those who are religion's severest critics—those who teach the eternity of the universe.

Maimonides therefore proved the existence of God in the man-ner of the Aristotelians. He did not rule out creation, but he freed the proof of the existence of God from dependence on it. As Maimonides explained it: "My method is as follows: the uni-verse is either eternal or has had a beginning. If it had a begin-ning there must necessarily exist a being who caused the beginning. This is clear to common sense. For a thing that has had a begin-ning, cannot be the cause of its own beginning (another must have caused it). The universe was, therefore, created by God. If, on the other hand, the universe were eternal it could in various ways be proved that apart from the things which constitute the universe, there exists a being which is neither a body nor a force in a body and which is one, eternal and immutable. That being is God. . . . I do not believe in that eternity but I wish to es-tablish the principle of the existence of God by an indisputable proof and should not like to see this most important principle founded on a basis which everyone could shake or attempt to demolish, and which others might consider was not being es-tablished at all."

Maimonides proved the existence of God, as did the Aris-totelians, from the impossibility of infinite motion. Assuming that the universe is eternal, then we must account for an eternal life process, for an infinite cycle of "becoming," for endless motion.

But an eternal movement implies an eternal mover, for motion is not self-generating; it depends on some one or something to start the movement. We must thus assume the existence of a first cause. God is the cause of all the motions of the universe, or its eternal mover. In the text of Maimonides this proof is elaborately drawn; and he cites twenty-six propositions taught by Aristotle which are assumed in it. The last of these propositions is the eternity of the universe which he is careful to explain he accepts "as a hypothesis only, for the purpose of demonstrating our theory."

God Is Absolute Being

The conception of God as the eternal mover of the universe yields for Maimonides a number of crucial inferences. It suggests that God is Absolute Being, that He is not subject to actions from causes beyond Himself and surely not dependent on them. For any being that is acted on by causes outside himself is transcended by those causes and is to that extent inferior to them; and such a being cannot be the prime mover of the total life of the universe.

These considerations also yield another vital inference—God's incorporeality. All corporeal things are composite; they are made up of a number of elements. It follows that were God a body He would be a composite, and thus He would not be Absolute Being. For He would owe His existence to His constituent elements as well as to the cause responsible for bringing those elements together into composition.

Another inference which derives from this reasoning is God's unity. If there were more than one Divine Being, each would have to be a composite. Such a "God" would have to consist of at least two elements, one which made him a "God," and one which differentiated him from the other "Gods." God Who is Absolute Being cannot be conceived as a composite.[1]

The unity of God was a time honored doctrine in Judaism, but His incorporeality was by no means as clearly established. The Biblical allusions to God in corporeal terms tended to suggest that God was a bodily being, more exalted no doubt than the bodies we know, but still endowed with physical organs, and subject to actions and passions not unlike those we know in human life. Thus there were many who conceived God as a magnified human person.

Maimonides fought uncompromisingly against this naive conception of God. He had his own interpretation for those Biblical passages which seemed to suggest that God was corporeal, and we shall have occasion to study them in our discussion of the Maimonidean theory of Revelation. But he made the rejection of notions involving God's corporeality an indispensable part of one's duty as a Jew. He branded those who entertained notions involving God's corporeality as gross sinners, and he heaped upon them verbal abuse—an unusual procedure for the usually calm Maimonides, but clearly indicative of his deep feelings on the subject. "Bear in mind," Maimonides wrote at the conclusion of a long discussion on this theme "that by the belief in the corporeality or in anything connected with corporeality you would provoke God . . . become His foe, His enemy, and His adversary to a higher degree than by the worship of idols. If you think that there is an excuse for those who believe in the corporeality of God on the ground of their training, their ignorance or their defective comprehension, you must make the same concession to the worshippers of idols; their worship is due to ignorance or to early training, 'they continue in the custom of their fathers' (Hullin 13a). You will perhaps say that the literal interpretation of the Bible causes men to fall into that doubt, but you must know that idolators were likewise brought to their belief by false imaginations and ideas. There is no excuse whatever for those who, being unable to think for themselves, do not accept (the doctrine of the incorporeality of God) from the true philosophers. I do not consider men as infidels who are unable to prove the incorporeality but I hold those to be so who do not believe it, especially when they see that Onkelos and Jonathan avoid (in reference to God) expressions implying corporeality as much as possible."[2]

Onkelos and Jonathan, here cited by Maimonides, are traditionally revered translators of the Bible into Aramaic. Both show a
tendency to soften the Biblical expressions ascribing corporeality
to God. Neither engages in the formal expositions of doctrine,
but they clearly show a repugnance to conceiving God as having a
bodily form. These were popular works, and they should have
led even the common people to avoid thinking of God as
corporeal.

God's Essence Is Unknowable

The doctrine that God is Absolute Being, incorporeal and
unitary, carried with it far-reaching implications. As Maimonides
saw it, it involved the renunciation of all attempts to know what
God is like. It involved the surrender of all attempts to achieve
a positive knowledge concerning God.

God is beyond definition. A definition, if it is to characterize
the true essence of an object, is by its very nature a composite.
It characterizes its object by reference to the genus and the differ-
entia; it classifies its object into a general category, as part of the
group with which it has most in common, and then places it
into a specific category, which endows it with its distinctive
qualities. God Whose existence is Absolute and Who is not dependent on causes beyond Himself, cannot be a composite.

God is beyond any descriptive attributes. Every attribute is an
"accident," a change which has happened to any being; and
God is not subject to change. Thus we cannot describe God by
the attribute of quality. "He is not a magnitude that any quality
resulting from quantity as such could be possessed by Him;—
He is not affected by external influences and therefore does not
possess any quality from emotion. He is not subject to physical
conditions and therefore does not possess strength or similar qualities; He is not an animate being, that He should have a certain
disposition of the soul, or acquire certain properties, as meekness,
modesty, etc., or be in a state to which animate beings as such are
subject as, for instance, in that of health or of illness. Hence it

follows that no attribute coming under the head of quality in its widest sense, can be predicated of God."

There are attributes of relationship—relationships of time or space or relationships to other beings—but they too are obviously inapplicable to God. Time and space relationships imply corporeality. For time is a concomitant of motion; it measures the successive positions of a moving body. It is a state in which only material objects can be in. And the same obviously applies to spatial relations. As to a possible relationship to other beings— that surely cannot be assumed of God. Relations can exist only between commensurates, between beings that have something in common to each other. God has nothing in common with other beings. His existence is Absolute, while theirs is dependent on causes beyond themselves.

Even what the philosophers call essential attributes, those which are part and parcel of the very concept of a human being,— existence, life, power, wisdom, will—cannot be applied to God, at least not in the sense in which we normally employ those terms.

As they appear in normal human discourse, these attributes also represent accidents which have occurred in the life of any being. Thus life and power and wisdom are not inherent in a person; they have developed in him. In God, however, they are included in His essence. God "is not a substance to which existence is joined as an accident, as an additional element. Consequently God exists without possessing the attribute of existence. Similarly, He lives without possessing the attribute of life, knows without possessing the attribute of knowledge . . . All this reduces itself to the one and the same entity; there is no plurality in Him."

Maimonides allowed the use of the "essential attributes" with reference to God, provided it was clear that they were identical with His essence, and were not something apart from it.

All We Can Say About God

The identification of the essential attributes with God's very essence as here formulated by Maimonides was a triumph for his power of subtle distinction, but it left problems that called for an answer. Is that all one might say about God? How remote God would become to us if we were thus forced to inhibit our speech and our thought! Scripture certainly allows itself to speak about God with profuse attributes. In the language of Scripture almost every attribute applied to human life—at least every attribute that denotes perfection—is freely ascribed to God. The identification of these attributes with God's essence, which of course destroys their character as real attributes seems like an altogether pointless performance. The assertion for example that God knows but not according to knowledge, since "His knowledge is His essence and His essence is His knowledge" tells us very little about God. If all that might possibly be predicated of Him must be identical with His essence, then we have destroyed the significance of the assertion. The terms thus predicated of God remain as unknown as His essence. There is no more enlightenment in such an assertion than there would be in the statement God is God. We do not know God's essence, and we cannot know what is identical with it.

Maimonides here developed two corollary ideas to the doctrine of attributes. We may employ positive attributes as Scripture does, but take them as characterizing not God Himself, as an essence, but His actions. There is a type of knowledge available to us about a being when we grasp the principles by which he functions in the universe. Thus we can gain a body of important knowledge concerning God by discerning His workings in the processes of existence. By analogy to our workings in the various tasks we perform in the world, we can fashion metaphors descriptive of God's work. Thus we meet the needs of human discourse. We can speak about God, and speak of Him where we normally have occasion to be concerned with Him—in the vast phenomena of existence in which we meet Him as a functioning cause. We may for instance speak of God as merciful, because of the apparent provision which we note in the life process to preserve every being and to endow it with the means of its growth and development. The term "merciful" is then a characterization not of God's essence, but of the quality of His providence.

The application of the essential attributes to God though they are all identical with His essence, Maimonides adds in a second important corollary to his main idea, has an important function— it enables us to negate imperfections in God. Every affirmative proposition about God is to be taken as the denial of a corresponding negative proposition. Maimonides particularized his doctrine by reference to eight descriptive terms, and they are arranged in such a way as to show how, when taken in the light of their negative implications, they offer us a well ordered exposition on the dissimilarity between God and all other beings. The first important declaration about God is that He exists, ruling out the notion that the universe is a self-sufficient enterprise and has its being without God. Then Maimonides offers the terms by which we may differentiate God's existence, from the existence of all other beings.

Thus we say God lives, and mean to distinguish Him from the sublunar elements, which are inanimate matter; we say He is incorporeal, differentiating Him from the celestial bodies which are corporeal; we say He is "from the beginning," thus differentiating Him from the immaterial intelligences which are due to a cause. Then we say He has power, wisdom and will, to deny the notion that He is incapable of producing things or that He is like some blind force acting by necessity, unconscious of its accomplishments, and devoid of any special design or purpose in its labors. The final term considered is unity, which Maimonides takes in the sense of uniqueness. Its significance is in its summation of all other negations, thus demonstrating that there is no other being comparable to God.

Negative attributes, Maimonides insists, are real attributes, and they convey valuable knowledge. They enable us to exclude false notions about God. They do not help us to know God's essence, but they are important. Considering the vast amount of misinformation and error which is so widely entertained about God, it becomes significant to make these assertions by which error can be boldly contradicted. We may not be able to know what God is, but it is important to know what He is not. The exclusion of false notions is an important phase of knowledge, though it does not probe into the divine essence, which must continue to elude our mortal minds.[3]

An Eternal or a Created Universe?

The negative attributes cited by Maimonides are a succinct statement of all his teachings concerning God. The first four, those which derive from existence, life, incorporeality, and eternity, only assert what he has proven with the aid of Aristotle, that there is a supreme Being Who has absolute existence. The three attributes which follow take us beyond philosophy and introduce us to what is distinctive in the doctrine of Maimonides. According to Aristotelians, God does not really perform any direct action; He does not produce anything. His role is that of the "first" mover of the universe and He generates these motions by drawing all things toward Himself. They are attracted toward Him because He is perfect. They move as the lover moves toward the object of his affection. God acts in this process as a kind of blind force, without design, without purpose. It was this Aristotelian notion which offered the greatest challenge to traditional religion. Maimonides rejected it as unwarranted by the facts as unsupported by the dictates of reason.

Maimonides offered the position of the Aristotelians a careful hearing, but he found their arguments wanting. Their doctrine assumed the eternity of the universe. They objected to creation by pointing to the world of common human experience where all production requires pre-existent materials, thus belying the notion of creation out of nothing as taught by the traditionalists.

They also argued that creation in time implies an infinite duration of God's inactivity—until the moment when He decided to
assume the role of Creator. This, they reasoned, is impossible,
for it takes an external cause to change the potential into the
actual producer of anything. In God we cannot assume potentialities waiting to be actualized in time, as we cannot conceive of
Him being subject to the action of causes beyond Himself. But
all this, Maimonides pointed out, was reasoning by analogy. It
assumes that the character of the production process within an
existent universe must necessarily parallel the process by which the
universe originally came into being. It assumes that God in com-
mencing an action must necessarily be governed by the same facts
which govern man, when he commences an action. Such reasoning is fallacious. God and man are totally dissimilar and we cannot draw analogies between them. The doctrine of eternity is
thus only a hypothesis; it cannot be proven. That in itself was
no argument for creation. But if eternity is not a clearly demonstrated truth, need we abandon what is so crucial to us in our
religious life to appease its advocates?

Maimonides also had positive arguments against the eternalists.
The universe, as they pictured it, was the result of a divine emanation; it was eternal because the process of emanation had gone
on eternally. But emanation was a natural process and subject to
the laws of natural causality. In every process of natural causation
there must be a correspondence between cause and effect; there
cannot be any elements in the effect which were not also present
in the cause. Thus "a form cannot emanate from matter nor
matter from form . . . the compound can only emanate from a
compound." How did the material world then arise? How explain
the leap from the immaterial to the material?

The naturalists assume that the only factor at work in the
universe are the necessities of nature which act with never failing
regularity and uniformity; and reason is supposed to be able to
detect these regularities and thus to account for the way events
transpire. The Aristotelians derived the events in the mundane

world from the influences of the celestial, but the celestial world itself defied an explanation based solely on the laws of natural causality. The variety of the spheres and stars, their number, their diverse positions and motions—these cannot be accounted for by the simple theories of naturalism. These phenomena suggest design and will, which is the capacity to conceive a desire at a particular time and to implement it in a particular way. The universe we behold reveals reason, and in its preponderant character can be accounted for by reason; and these elements of reason point to the existence of an intelligent first cause. But it also reveals elements which are beyond reason, elements which suggest a free Being at work to carry out the terms of His will. These elements suggest that the first cause is a free Creator, who works as He wills, and designs as He chooses.[4]

There is a Realm of Nature

The Maimonidean rejection of naturalism did not mean a repudiation of order in nature. There was a school of theologians, the Moslem sect known as the Ashariya, who entertained such a view. They were apologists for traditional religion, and they based their doctrine on the total denial of a realm of nature, where events proceed with uniformity, and by principles inherent in their being. They saw all reality as constituted of atoms, which in themselves have no fixed properties to act or to evoke actions from one another. Left to themselves these atoms would comprise a chaotic, inert mass. The existence of the universe, and of coherent events in it, reflected for them the direct intervention of God. The universe in itself reflects no inherent principles of rationality. Its being is an ever-renewing act of God's will, and must be looked upon as a constant miracle. Thus, the reduction of existence to chaos, the elimination from it of its own inherent elements of order, helped them demonstrate the existence of God, who is the ever-present and all pervading Creator and Sustainer of all things.

For Maimonides the universe revealed not only God's will but also His wisdom. For him nature is a coherent whole; the universe is a unitary being, constituted of inter-dependent parts which integrate harmoniously, one complementing the other. There are fixed properties in things, and nature is a realm of being wherein one may detect order, uniformity and rationality. God transcends nature; He is its architect; it is He who conferred upon it its uniformities. And God respects those uniformities, simply because He is not a capricious being. Thus we do not ascribe to God "the power of doing what is impossible," as controverting the rules of mathematics. He wills what is possible, and His will is in accordance with His wisdom. Theoretically God could change the nature of an organism, but "it has never been His will to do it, and it never will be." Maimonides affirmed His conviction that the universe is constant and "perpetually with the same properties with which the Creator has endowed it, and that none of these will ever be changed although the Creator has the power to change the whole universe, to annihilate or to remove any of its properties." Maimonides carried his conviction to the extent of accepting the indestructability of the universe. Once formed the universe will persist as it is, with the same properties, for all time. It will not perish, as was believed in the popular theology of his time.

Miracles Are Possible

Maimonides' doctrine of nature enabled him to affirm the possibility of miracles. If natural necessity, working with never-failing regularity, were the sole condition of events in the universe, we could not entertain the belief in miracles. But there is a Being above nature who is free to carry out what He wills. We cannot conceive that He would permanently alter the properties of things. That would introduce anarchy into the universe. But miracles represent no permanent change in the nature of things. They are temporary modifications, introduced by God, whenever He sees fit to do so, to enact His purpose in the universe. Maimonides re-interpreted many of the miracle stories in Scrip-

ture, and he sought to minimize their scope. But as to the possibility of miracles he was unequivocally clear. They are consistent
with a rational view of the universe. There is law and order
and reason manifest in nature, but not total determinism; and
miracles are thus possible.[5]

Angels and Forces of Nature

The instruments through which God effects His work in the
universe are immaterial forces, which Maimonides identified with
the angels mentioned in the Bible. Each being, he held, plays its
part in the scheme of cosmic life, not through the direct contact
of God, but through the impulsion of a distinctive force inherent
in its nature. From the spheres above, to the tiniest organism
below, existence unfolds through the energizing activity of an
indwelling impulse or force which presses it on to a fulfillment
of its destiny, and which has been implanted there by God for
that very purpose. In human life, angelic activity is illustrated
in the entire realm of "the natural and psychical forces of an
individual." But the same activity is at play wherever life asserts
itself. As Maimonides generalized: "All parts of the universe, even
the limbs of animals in their actual form, are produced through
angels; for natural forces and angels are identical."

Scripture frequently refers to angels as corporeal beings, but
that is the work of imaginative personification; as forces inherent
in physical organisms they are necessarily immaterial. Maimonides
was aware that for the unsophisticated his conception of angels
would sound shockingly unfamiliar. They preferred to picture
angels in fantastically corporeal terms and as miracle working
emissaries of God who were wholly above the natural order.

Maimonides satirized all this as the credulity of ignorance,
all the more pathetic since it frequently appears in the ranks of
those high in the religious community. "How bad and injurious
is the blindness of ignorance," he exclaimed. "Say to a person
who is believed to belong to the wise men of Israel that the Al-
mighty sends His angels to enter the womb of a woman and to

form there the foetus, he will be satisfied with the account; he will believe it, and even find in it a description of God's might and wisdom; although he believes that the angel consists of burning fire, and is as big as a third part of the universe, yet he considers it possible as a divine miracle. But tell him that God gave the seed a formative power which produces and shapes the limbs, and that this power is called 'angel . . .' and he will turn away; because he cannot comprehend the true greatness and power of creating forces that act in a body without being perceived by the senses."[6]

The Rationality and the Mystery of the Universe

We have noted that the ascription by Maimonides of design and will to God, and the power of free creation, was in negative rather than in positive terms. The attributes in question—power, wisdom and will—were positive in their formulation, but their real meaning was negative. Maimonides remained consistent with this doctrine. Having affirmed design in the universe he is careful to assert that the character of the design remains unclear. It eludes human understanding. We may, in other words, render the position of Maimonides thus: the character of the universe is such that we cannot consider it the work of a blind force, operating without design or will. God's activity, "is not like that of the fire in producing heat, or that of the sun in sending forth light, but consists in constantly giving them stability and order by well-established rule." But the principles of that rule, the ultimate nature of the design—the ultimate final cause of things —we do not know. But, added Maimonides, neither do the naturalists know the ultimate meaning of things.

Amidst all its rationality, the universe is permeated with mystery, which our little minds cannot unravel. Thus we cannot know why God created the universe at a particular time rather than another, or why He saw fit to give existence the specific form which He chose to give it rather than any other. Nor can we know how God acts to sustain the universe and to bring into being the varied enterprises of its life.

We may draw on various analogies to help portray the character of divine activity. We may think of the universe as a mighty boat or a chariot, with God as the one who rides upon it and steers it on its course. We may also think of God as the intellect of the universe, who functions in the cosmic process as the intellect functions in human life. But none of these give us any real clue to the nature of God's creative processes.

The principal difficulty in grasping the nature of God's activity is to reconcile the paradox of His transcendence and His immanence. Thus the conception of God as the intellect of the universe is an imperfect analogy, among other things, because in man the faculty of thinking is a force inherent in the body and is not separate from it, while God inheres and at the same time transcends the visible universe. "How God rules the universe and provides for it is a complete mystery; man is unable to solve it. For, on the one hand, it can be proved that God is separate from the universe, and in no contact whatever with it; but on the other hand, His rule and providence can be proved to exist in all parts of the universe, even the smallest."

Surely, we cannot know the final why of creation. Thus if we assume with Aristotle that the universe is eternal, what more can we see in the life process than the universal struggle to perpetuate and improve the form of each species? Natural science "investigates into the object of everything in nature," and it helps to reveal the intelligence and design in individual organisms, "but it does not speak of the ultimate final cause . . . ." The final why which the heart longs to know our sciences cannot answer for us.

If we assume that the universe was created in time by God, what more can we say? There are those who maintain that the purpose of creation is the emergence of man, who was formed that he might serve God. But could not man have been produced without some of the objects in creation; and if so, what is the purpose of those objects? "Even if the universe existed for man's sake and man existed for the purpose of serving God, the question remains, what is the end of serving God? . . . It might perhaps be replied that the service of God is intended for our own perfection . . . But what is the object of our being perfect? We must at last arrive at the answer. It was the will of God, or His wisdom decreed it; and this is the correct answer." But the nature of that divine wisdom "we are unable to comprehend." With all our theorizing therefore we can say no more than this: "It is not unreasonable to assume that the works of God, their existence and preceding non-existence, are the result of His wisdom, but we are unable to understand many of the ways of His wisdom in His works."

Our knowledge is, at best, a dull flame that illumines only a fragment of the great darkness that surrounds our lives, and we must be content to cherish that. "All that we understand is the fact that He exists, that He is a Being to whom none of His creatures is similar, who has nothing in common with them, who does not include plurality, who is never too feeble to produce other beings, and whose relation to the universe is that of a steerman to a boat; and even this is not a real relation, a real simile, but serves only to convey to us the idea that God rules the universe; that is, that He gives it duration, and preserves its necessary arrangement . . . Praised be He! In the contemplation of His essence, our comprehension and knowledge prove insufficient, in the examination of His works, how they necessarily result from His will, our knowledge proves to be ignorance, and in the endeavor to extol Him in words, all our efforts in speech are mere weakness and failure."[7]

A fresh examination of the issues has enabled Maimonides to fashion a conception of God which avoids the extremes of traditionalism and of naturalism. It retains all the elements that are really crucial in traditional religion, and is consistent with the valid demands of the life of reason.

Chapter IV

RELIGION IN CULTURE

The religion which Maimonides defended was not only a set of doctrines. It was a definite way of life. It had its code of law; it had its sacred Scripture which taught certain ideas about God and man, that did not always jibe with the philosophical conceptions, as he advanced them; it had its own way to God— prayer, religious ceremony in home and synagogue. How did all this fit in with the notion that only through philosophy can we rise to closeness with God? If religion was to meet the challenge of the times, it was necessary to defend it as an institution in culture, and not only as another version of a philosophy of the universe.

The Meaning of Prophecy

The key to the Maimonidean defense of institutional religion was his doctrine of prophecy. For many the belief in prophecy was the acceptance of God's capricious interruption in the flow of life in the universe. The prophet was a person upon whom almost magical powers had been conferred from on high. The prophets were like sooth-sayers who could predict the future. They reported fantastic tales which could not be accounted for by any canons of reason or of knowledge such as ordinary mortals possessed. The belief in prophetic revelations was in a sense the antithesis of the life of reason, and of the pursuit of knowledge through science and philosophy. Maimonides dismissed this notion, and placed prophecy within the realm of an intelligible interpretation of life. Prophecy is not reason; the prophetic experience is quite different from the act of logical demonstration; but prophecy is not an irrational phenomenon. Indeed, it is a vital complement to the life of reason and offers man invaluable truths which he could not attain by reason alone.

The achievement of knowledge, according to Maimonides, is always a cooperative effort. Man uses his faculties to perceive, but he is dependent on stimulation from a source of knowledge beyond himself. That was good Aristotelian psychology. Among the cosmic beings which Aristotle recognized as part of the hierarchy of the universe was the Active Intellect. It was an immaterial force, an Intelligence which received its influence from God and transmitted it to the earth, thus generating the movement and life on our planet. But the Active Intellect is also the source from which knowledge streams upon our minds. The mind is only a potential knower; it is the influence of the Active Intellect, in which there is all truth as an actual reality that activizes our own intellects and begets the knowledge to which mortal minds may attain. Knowledge is thus in some respects an illumination from above, even as it is the fruit of our own seeking.[1]

Prophecy is another form of illumination from above. It is an illumination concerning the nature of things, concerning the truths about God and about human destiny. In its most familiar form prophecy appears in the experience of a "call" which impels certain people to perform heroic deeds in the service of some good cause or to become creative in the fields of theology, politics, science or literature. Maimonides describes this "call" of prophecy in vivid and familiar terms: "A person feels as if something came upon him, and as if he received a new power that encourages him to speak. He treats of science or composes hymns, exhorts his fellow-men, discusses political and theological problems; all this he does while awake and in full possession of his senses." Some books of the Bible such as Psalms, Proverbs, Daniel, Job and Chronicles clearly reflect this expression of prophecy.

This is, however, only a lower form of prophecy. In its fullest, prophecy is a much deeper experience; it occurs in a vision or a dream, and it may be accompanied by the vision of angelic beings, by the hearing of voices, by the appearance of various symbols with or without their interpretation. In the course of his experience the prophet may find himself holding discourse with the angels; he may hear God addressing him; and a divine light will shine for him. All through this experience, the normal functioning of the body is suspended; a great bodily agitation ensues; and an immense illumination lights up the mind, as a flash of lightning lights up the darkness of the surrounding night. What normally requires laborious reasoning, and, indeed, what laborious reasoning cannot establish, is grasped intuitively and with an overpowering sense of certainty. The experiences of Ezekiel and Zachariah, so vividly described in the Bible, illustrate prophecy on this level.[2]

The manner in which the divine influence is exerted on the prophet we do not know. The Bible describes the prophet as receiving his message through a speech process. That however is only a metaphor, intended to make this phenomenon more comprehensible to people who know no other form of communications. "When we are told that God addressed the prophets and spoke to them, our minds are merely to receive a notion that there is a divine knowledge to which the prophets attain; we are to be impressed with the idea that the things which the prophets communicate to us come from the Lord, and are not altogether the products of their own conceptions and ideas." Even when the prophets hear voices, these voices are not the direct utterances of God. They are "created" voices of which God is the first cause, as He is the first cause of all things in existence. But God is not corporeal and He does not act in the manner of corporeal beings.[3]

Prophecy, like any other attainment of knowledge, commences with the divine influence, which moves through the Active Intellect and then descends upon man. Prophecy differs from other forms of attaining knowledge only in the intensity of the influence which reaches man and in the participation of a mental faculty in addition to the intellect which is not involved in the case of other acquisitions of knowledge. That faculty is an active imagination.

The intellect acts in the prophetic experience as it acts in the process of reason. It formulates concepts. Because of the intensity of the action involved in this form of illumination, these concepts will form more readily, eliminating many intermediate steps on which the process of reason normally depends. Because this intensity derives from the great bounty of the influence exerted, the prophet's illumination is more potent even in relation to the volume of truth received. But for the prophetic experience to run its full course, there must also come into play the prophet's imagination.

The imagination particularizes the concepts which have appeared in what we may call the purely intellectual phase of prophecy. It expresses them by symbols and illustrations. It projects them into vivid and concrete images, giving them a forceful and dramatic quality. Out of the imaginative play upon these concepts, the unformed future comes closer, and the specific events involving them, take shape and become discernible to the eye of intuition. The symbols, the angelic beings, the divine voices which figure in the Biblical stories of the prophets' experiences, are all creations of the imagination. The significance of this imaginative elaboration of the truth is to make it more comprehensible to the common man. The truth as formulated in intellectual concepts is abstract and therefore remote from the average mind. It becomes more cogent as it becomes more concretized, through the action of the imagination, endowing it with a vivid and pictorial quality.

The essential prerequisites for prophecy are thus the intellect and the imagination. Prophecy is not a capricious event which transpires among people without reference to their qualifications. The prophet must have a highly perfected intellect and a highly perfected imagination. The perfection of the intellect is something a person can attain through training, for it is a matter of acquiring wisdom and knowledge. The prerequisite imagination is largely a matter of endowment. It depends on the quality of a bodily organ, the brain, and it is not materially affected by training.

The imagination is, however, affected by a person's moral and emotional life. The imagination generally acts in line with a person's serious interests. Thus a person may have great intellectual attainments but if he loves wealth or power or pleasure, his imagination will not be concerned with the acquisition of truth. As Maimonides put it: "It is a well-known fact that the thing which engages greatly and earnestly man's attention whilst he is awake and in the full possession of his senses forms during his sleep (or vision) the object of the action of his imaginative faculty. Imagination is then only influenced by the intellect insofar as it is predisposed for such influence."

The imagination will also be affected by the emotional life. A prophet's vision will be obstructed by intense grief or anger. Even the experienced prophet, and even one who has all the requisite formal qualifications will find his prophetic powers gone when in the wake of illness or of some personal or social tragedy, he becomes demoralized and loses his self-mastery. A serene, poised, well-balanced disposition is a necessary prerequisite for the imagination to do its work properly and thus to aid in creating the prophetic experience.

Because prophecy is enacted by means of human faculties which differ in their states of perfection, the prophetic experience varies with individual prophets. "As we have in wisdom one wise man greater than another, so do we have in prophecy, one prophet greater than another." Some may receive prophecies sufficient to broaden their own understanding, but insufficient to becoming protagonists of those prophecies before the world. With others a more intense experience sends them forth into the world as unyielding champions of the truth. With some prophecy will come irregularly and on infrequent occasions. With others it will come more frequently and more regularly.

In one of the most vivid passages of the *Moreh*, Maimonides thus describes the varying degrees of prophetic illumination: "At times the truth shines so brilliantly that we perceive it as clear as day. Our nature and habit then draw a veil over our perception and we return to a darkness almost as dense as before . . . On some the lightning flashes in rapid succession and they seem to be in continuous light. Some perceive the prophetic flash at long intervals . . . By others only once during the whole night is a flash of lightning perceived . . . Others are in the condition of men whose darkness is illuminated not by lightning but by some kind of crystal or similar stone or other substance that possesses the property of shining during the night; and to them even this small amount of light is not continuous, but now it shines and now it vanishes."

When all these factors are present, the prerequisites for prophecy have been fulfilled. For there is always a divine influence in action. Like gushing waters of a living fountain, knowledge and insight are flowing eternally from God's being. It takes, however, sensitive spirits, duly qualified people to receive the influence. When they are available, then we have in operation all the underlying causes that beget prophecy.

Prophecy follows every other phenomenon in the universe; it conforms to the law of causality. It is not an unaccounted for appearance breaking in upon the scheme of things. However, causality as Maimonides saw it, is not the sole factor in the making of events. God retains freedom to act outside the laws of causality in the performance of miracles, for example. It thus transpires that not every person who is qualified prophesies. The failure of qualified people to experience prophetic illumination is a kind of miracle. There can be no prophecy without qualification for it, but there may be the qualification without bringing on prophecy.[4]

Prophecy is universal; it is not confined to any one people or to any one religious community. But God, exercising His free initiative has seen fit to guide prophecy toward a well-defined line of development. While there have been prophets among other peoples, it is in Israel that the great prophets have spoken. Examining the writings of the prophets, moreover, we find that prophecy has aimed toward a specific goal of human enlightenment. The core of prophetic truth appears in the writings of Moses who was the greatest of the prophets. There were prophets who preceded him and others who followed him, but it is in his career that prophecy achieved its supreme manifestation. Indeed, Moses so outranked the other prophets that his designation by the same title becomes misleading, and the term "prophet" when applied to him is really a homonym. In contradiction to other prophets to whom illumination came occasionally, he enjoyed a continuous illumination. And he was so at home in the constant light, that there was no bodily reaction to his experience. Thus his imagination was not a factor in the process, and what he saw remained in a state of intellectual purity, without being pictorialized. Moreover he was so completely emancipated from the claims of his bodily nature that he functioned veritably as a disembodied intelligence. As such he communed with God directly, without the mediation of the Active Intellect.

Because of his unique prophetic powers, Moses was able to do what no other prophet had done before him—he promulgated the *Torah* in which all the beliefs and practices essential to the perfection of mankind, for all time to come, found their expression. Other prophets functioned as teachers and preachers; they exhorted their fellow-men to the truth as they saw it. But they did not see themselves as the emissaries of a divine law which was to be enjoined upon all men.

Certain religious laws and customs had their origin in pre-Mosaic times. But the pre-Mosaic prophets who established them sought to benefit their own immediate family circle. They did not seek to give those laws universal scope. Abraham, for instance, performed the rite of circumcision upon himself and those of his household, "but he did not address his fellow-men prophetically on this subject." And those laws are authoritative in Judaism only because they were reaffirmed in the Torah of Moses. Thus the rite of circumcision is to be practiced because the Mosaic law calls for it, not because Abraham instituted it.

The work of Moses was likewise decisive in relation to the prophets who followed him. They were primarily concerned with exhorting people to obey the Mosaic law or with criticizing them when they strayed from it. Their work was at no time a departure from what had been instituted by Moses.[5]

The Mosaic law exists on two levels, the written and the so-called "oral Torah." The Pentateuch, which is the written Torah, includes the more general norms of law and doctrine. An accompanying body of interpretations and elaborations were transmitted simultaneously as oral tradition. In time the oral tradition was reduced to writing as well, and it is the foundation of Talmudic literature. Taken together, this Mosaic law constitutes a body of doctrine and practice by which all mankind can steer itself to its true end.

The Mosaic law is an unchanging law, intended to be permanently binding in its authority. Post-Mosaic teachers could, however, continue to create a literature of interpretation based on the teachings of Moses, and they were equally free to make independent expressions in moral or doctrinal matters, where they did not conflict with the Mosaic teachings. Moreover, where they did not clash with the Mosaic law, later authorities were free to enact new legislation. Such new legislation might be in the form of independent enactments or through deduction from Mosaic precedents, by a special system of hermeneutics which Moses taught as part of his oral communication. This new legislation was authoritive but it was known as "rabbinic" rather than as Mosaic in character.

Under conditions of emergency, too, individual prophets or rabbinic courts could temporarily suspend the Mosaic law. "Whether it be to suspend a positive commandment or to transgress a negative commandment," declared Maimonides, "if its purpose is to bring great numbers back to the faith or to spare many Israelites from stumbling over other pitfalls, they (the rabbinic authorities) are authorized to ordain so, in accordance with the demands of the times. As the physician may amputate a person's hand or foot in order to save his life, so may the rabbinic authorities sanction at times the temporary suspension of some religious laws so that the system of religious law as a whole shall survive. In the words of the sages (Shabbat 151b): 'If it is a matter of healing an ill person, desecrate the Sabbath so that he may live to observe many Sabbaths.' "[6]

There is ample evidence behind the prophecy of Moses, Maimonides explained, to authenticate its genuineness. According to tradition, all Israelites were present at the divine revelation before Mt. Sinai from which issued the ten commandments, and there they watched Moses as he communed with God. Because prophecy requires a high degree of intellectual perfection as a prerequisite, we cannot assume that the people as a whole shared in that experience. The significance of their presence at Sinai was not in their active participation, but in their serving as witnesses, to attest to the genuineness of the event in which Moses alone was the central figure. The people heard and saw what transpired but they did not comprehend it. Moses alone received the message and then conveyed it to the people.[7]

True and False Prophets

Maimonides succeeded in bringing the subject of prophecy within the range of intelligible experience. But he was aware of one important difficulty in his theory. The phenomenon which he called prophecy is familiar, but how can we trust the truths which emerge from it? The fact is that there have been men in history who have gone through such experiences, and have brought to the world not liberating truth but gross error. Maimonides had no difficulty in explaining the deceptions, the hallucinations frequently arising in the very experiences which by all external signs should be experiences of prophecy. Individuals with limited intellects and keen imaginations are bound to beget confusion and distorted notions in their experiences of "illumination." An active imagination unchecked by a sound intellect is bound to lead people astray. But how are we to distinguish between the true and false prophet? Unless we can differentiate between the two, how can we depend on any prophet and follow his doctrine in the confidence that it is true?

The subjective character of the prophetic experience make it easy, moreover, for imposters to appear and to offer themselves as true emissaries of God. Many a would-be prophet has proven to be a pretender if not an innocent victim of his own hallucinations. Some may even "plagiarize the word of others and proclaim things which, no doubt, have been said by God, that is to say, have been the subjects of divine inspiration, but not to them." Maimonides therefore undertook a definition of various criteria for distinguishing the true prophet from the false.

Maimonides suggested various tests by which to judge claims to prophecy. The performance of miracles is no criterion; the so-called miracles may be feats of magic. One test, Maimonides taught, is the character of the claimant to prophecy. To earn our respectful consideration we must know him to be of a noble character and of high intellectual endowments. "We must examine the merits of the person, obtain an accurate account of his actions, and consider his character. The best test is the rejection, abstention and contempt of bodily pleasures; for this is the first condition of men and, *a fortiore,* of prophets." The sensuality in a pretender to prophecy is the means by which God "exposes false prophets to public shame, in order that those who really seek the truth may really find it, and not err or go astray."

Another test is a study of the prophetic message in the light of subsequent events. The prophet is essentially a teacher of moral and religious doctrine. In its more significant form his message is a clue to the future. When the future vindicates his predictions, we have a confirmation of his prophetic status; when the future fails to vindicate his prediction he is exposed as a false prophet. This is particularly true if the prediction concerned favorable developments. The divine forgiveness may withhold an impending doom foreseen by the prophet; and when history does not precipitate an expected disaster, the prophet's standing may not be impugned. On the other hand, we may be certain that the false optimists of history who have spoken with prophetic pretensions are imposters or madmen; they are not true prophets.

Another test is an objective examination of the contents in the message proclaimed by the would-be prophet. His message must not contradict what has been established by reason. If, for instance, a claimant to prophecy would sanction any form of idol worship, we do not even examine any "signs" he might have to offer in confirmation of his mission; we know he speaks falsehood. "The mind that contradicts his testimony is more reliable than the eye that beholds his signs. For it has been demonstrated by rational proof by philosophers that one must not revere or worship except Him who is the source of all existing things and in Whom is joined every type of perfection."

The claimant to prophecy must also conform to what is ordained in the established prophetic teachings preceding him. He speaks falsehood for instance if he calls for any breaks with the prescriptions of the Mosaic law. A prophet may call for temporary adjustments in traditional law, if circumstances warrant it. But he must not call for its formal modification. Since the Mosaic revelation is the highest manifestation of prophecy, any departure from it would represent a deterioration, and God would surely not authorize it.[8]

In Defense of the Torah

The interpretation of prophecy was for Maimonides a prelude to the defense of the Torah. In his traditional religion, the Torah held a position of primacy. It was the embodiment of all truth, the most revered possession of the Jewish people. But the teachings of the Torah seemed so different from the conception of religion which Maimonides himself advocated. It was not concerned primarily with doctrinal matters at all. If the way to the true love of God is the way of reason, of science and philosophy, then what did the Torah offer us toward achieving this goal? The Torah concerns itself with action rather than with doctrine; it emphasizes ritual, ceremony and prayer; it abounds in narratives about ancient heroes; and it teaches a naive conception of God, ascribing to Him physical organs, and human emotions, as well as a kind of arbi-

trary intervention in the working of the universe which seems to
rule out an order of nature where events follow a logic of their
own, in conformity to the laws of cause and effect. What did this
have in common with religion as Maimonides had interpreted it,
in which reason was to play so crucial a role? How was the religion of the Torah to be efficacious in leading a man to God?

Maimonides defended the Torah as a necessary complement to
the truths which we may attain by reason. Its distinctive contribution is to offer man guidance in the areas of faith and life where
reason is not equipped to operate. As the fruit of prophetic illumination, the Torah represents a more penetrating, a more direct comprehension of the world as a whole. "Prophecy can teach
things beyond the reach of philosophical speculation." Thus the
most crucial of all problems in religion, the questions of whether
the universe is created or eternal, finds its decisive answer in the
Torah. For the Torah proclaims unequivocally that the universe
was created in time. This was the very crux of the issue between
naturalism and traditional religion. By its doctrine of creation, the
Torah has thus taken its stand against the notion that natural
determinism is the sole factor governing events in the universe—
a notion, which we have noted previously, negates all the vital
elements of religion as we know it.

There are certain truths which are fundamental to a man's life
in the world, such as the existence, the unity, the omniscience, the
will and the eternity of God. Philosophy can prove these doctrines
through its own methods, but shall we suspend life till reason do
her work of demonstration? These matters were too important to
be left to each individual to work out for himself by the aid of
the intellect. Some might never achieve it, or it would take too
long and precious time would be lost in the meanwhile. The
Torah therefore offers us these teachings categorically, without
argument, leaving the finer points elaborating each of these doctrines for reason to do later on, as a person matures in his intellectual powers. "Scripture only teaches the chief points of those
true principles which lead to the true perfection of man, and only

demands in general terms faith in them. All this is given in the form of final results but they cannot be understood fully and accurately except after the acquisition of many kinds of knowledge." These many kinds of knowledge, we have noted previously, included especially the studies of mathematics, astronomy, logic, and natural science. But it was a boon to human life that we must not depend upon the mastery of all this knowledge for the more immediate elements of doctrine, that the Torah makes them available to us as simple affirmations which can be accepted without going through the intricate processes of logical demonstration.

The Torah, likewise, concerns itself with morals, and seeks to guide man as to how he is to live in society. The most important contribution to human moralization in the Torah is the personalization of divine providence. This is achieved in the famous thirteen moral attributes of God which are elsewhere condensed to three: *hesed,* loving-kindness, *zedakah,* righteousness, and *mishpat,* judgment. All attributes of God are anthropomorphisms, since God is beyond positive characterizations, and surely beyond all emotions. These are really descriptions of how God's government of the universe appears to us. But they are ascribed to Him metaphorically, and thereby serve the cause of human moralization. For the moral attributes of God become patterns to model after, goals to emulate. And the rabbis indeed considered the quest to imitate God as the highest moral perfection in man.

The Torah serves the needs of a just society in an even more direct fashion. Maimonides cited the vast body of specific legislation by which the Torah sought to create a harmonious order of human relations and to establish justice among men. In addition, it reaches down to the nature of the common man, and prescribes certain truths "the belief in which is indispensable in perfecting our social relations; such is the belief that God is angry with those who disobey Him, for it leads to the fear and dread of disobeying Him." A morality motivated by pragmatic considerations is not the highest type of morality. When we have risen sufficiently in our development, we know to choose the good because it is good, and

to shun the evil because it is evil, without any interest in the rewards of this world or of the hereafter. We choose the good and
shun the evil because we model our lives after the manifestations
of divine providence. The quest to be godlike, to imitate His ways,
is a natural, disinterested quest for a spiritually mature person,
and rewards and punishments do not figure in it. But in the preliminary stages of human development the principle of retribution
is an important factor in man's moral motivations, and helps in
the creation of justice among men.[9]

The Torah, also, employs a highly effective pedagogy in pre-
senting these truths. Its language is vivid and simple. It concretizes
its ideas through profuse illustrations, in parables and metaphors.
Its doctrine of God, for example, is not stated in abstract, philosophic terms, but in terms drawn from common human experience,
which brings it within comprehension by most men. Maimonides
expressed it thus: "Expressions which can easily be comprehended
and understood by all, are applied to the Creator. Hence the description of God by attributes implying corporeality, in order to
express His existence; because the multitude of people do not
easily conceive existence unless in connection with a body, and that
which is not a body nor connected with a body has for them no
existence. Whatever we regard as a state of perfection, is likewise
attributed to God, as expressing that He is perfect in every respect
and that no imperfection or deficiency whatever is found in Him.
. . . In relation to God, what we consider to be a state of perfection is in truth the highest degree of imperfection. If, however,
men were to think that those human perfections were absent in
God, they would consider Him as imperfect."

The pedagogy of the Torah, moreover, reckons with the important truth of human nature that we learn more effectively by
example than by precept, and by action rather than by discussion.
It utilizes both these methods. It marshals historic personalities
who lived by the beliefs and practices which comprise its recommended pattern of life and others who defied that pattern. By
the example of their lives and the consequences which resulted

therefrom, it exhorts obedience to its mandates and forewarns dis-
obedience.

The Torah teaches by action through a series of disciplines built
around each major religious doctrine. By the "doing" of those
disciplines the doctrines are bound to register profoundly in the
consciousness of people. The awareness of God and of man's duties
to revere Him, for instance, are amply enforced through the elaborate practice of piety, of religious ritual and ceremony. The doctrine
of creation finds its most competent teacher in the observance of
the Sabbath. At the same time it combats every social custom and
every group habit which was in any way related to the beliefs or
practices of idolatry.[10]

The Torah, once more reckoning with the truths of human
nature, did not demand a sharp break with the habits of people,
adapting, where necessary, old culture patterns to its own ends
rather than asking that they be superseded. Thus the Torah retained the cult of animal sacrifices as a mode of worship. That
cult was universally prevalent in those days when the Torah was
promulgated, and it would have been too difficult for the people
to emancipate themselves from it. The Torah therefore retained
it, but purged it of all pagan elements. "By this divine plan it was
effected that the traces of idolatry were blotted out, and the truly
great principles of our faith, the existence and unity of God, were
firmly established. This result was thus obtained without deterring
or confusing the minds of people by the abolition of a service to
which they were accustomed and which alone was familiar to
them."

The Torah also provides a technique for disciplining our emotional natures, to train us in curbing our physical desires. This is
necessary in order to counteract the tendency to consider physical
enjoyment "as an object to be sought for its own sake." The Torah
accomplishes this end by such prescriptions as the law of diet and
the laws governing sex life. The forbidden foods, apart from
certain specific values which they have individually, "restrain the
growth of desire, the indulgence of seeking that which is pleasant

and the disposition to consider the appetite for eating and drinking as the end of man's existence." The laws regulating sex life aim "to restrain as much as possible indulgence in lust, and to teach that this enjoyment is not, as foolish people think, the final cause of man's existence." When we commit any excesses, moreover, the Torah offers us the therapeutic discipline of repentance by which we may heal our character defects. A virtuous character is cultivated through the acquisition of virtuous practices, and the Torah thus offers the necessary technique for this all important development.

A character so disciplined has conferred upon a person a double blessing. It has made him a better citizen, a more cooperative member of society, since good citizenship frequently calls for self-denial. The creation of justice in society requires that "we do not do simply as we please, desire or are able to do; but everyone of us does that which contributes to the common welfare." Self-denial, moreover, is essential to intellectual pusuits, the domain where lies man's highest perfection, since the love of comfort and pleasure will divert men from intellectual labors.

Maimonides finally called attention to the fact that in the elaboration of its moral disciplines, the Torah was careful not to impose undue hardships on people. It seeks to curb excesses, but it does not encourage ascetic withdrawals from life. Men of strong passions or of low moral inclination have found the way of life ordained in the Torah too hard. But they are not competent to judge. "We must not consider the law easy or hard as it appears to any wicked, low-minded, and immoral person, but as it appears to the judgment of the most perfect, who, according to the law, are fit to be the example for all mankind." If we thus judge the Torah, and see it from the perspective of the virtuous, we shall find it a perfect law, representing the happy medium between all objectionable extremes.[11]

The Torah thus meets the total needs of man. It differs from philosophy in that it deals with the problems of humanity as a whole, and not with a select few individuals. It also differs from systems of legislation that do not derive from prophetic inspiration. The latter concern themselves with man's physical perfection only; they endeavor to create a social order which will enable man to meet his physical needs. The Torah likewise concerns itself with the problems of man's physical perfection. It establishes a body of moral principles and practices calculated to enable men to fashion a just social order. But, in addition, it tries to disseminate correct doctrines. Indeed it places the social order in its proper perspective, as the base from which men may proceed, unimpeded by material wants, in accordance with the different levels of their intellectual powers, toward the acquisition of intellectual perfection where lies man's highest good.[12]

It is in this spirit that Maimonides interpreted—and justified—all the commandments of the Torah. With some (the so-called "judgments") he had little difficulty; their significance was readily apparent. There were however others (the "ordinances") whose purpose did not seem clear, as the prohibition of enjoying the fruit of a tree in its first three years or of a vineyard in which diverse seeds have grown (Lev. 19:23, Deut. 22:9). Maimonides was convinced that upon diligent investigation all Scriptural commandments will prove rationally justifiable. Thus, in the case of the "ordinances" we shall discover their rationality when we study them in their historical setting. Those practices and many others like them had been employed in various magic rites associated with ancient agriculture. The Torah prohibited them as part of its ancient struggle against idolatry and superstition. There is nothing vain and nothing irrational in the Torah. All the commandments, as Maimonides saw it, were designed to achieve specific benefits in human life. "Every one of the six hundred and thirteen precepts serve to inculcate some truth, to remove some erroneous opinion, to establish proper relations in society, to diminish evil, to train us in good manners, or to warn us against bad habits."[13]

An Outer and an Inner Truth

The Torah thus represents a guide to doctrine and life, adapted to the comprehension of the common man. The philosopher can sympathize with the need of reckoning with the intellectual powers of those who are to receive the truth, but does not adaptation create falsification? If in so many instances, the Torah employs a vocabulary and formulates its concepts to suit the limited capacities for knowledge among the masses of humanity, then it is not bringing us truth as it really is, which is the quest of the philosopher. From the point of view of the philosopher, the Torah thus tends to be regarded as a text of inferior worth, addressed to the uneducated, and teaching a religion which his own more highly developed intellect cannot accept.

Maimonides denied this. The prophets simplified the truth for the common man, but they did not falsify it for the philosopher. How could they do both, convey an "adapted" truth for the uneducated, and the full truth for the educated? They performed this formidable task by developing a style of their own—which is the distinctive literary style of the Bible. It conveys its message on two levels. It employs a language which reveals a little and conceals a little, a language of hints, of allegories and parables, of metaphors and homonyms. The literal meaning is addressed to the common people, while the hidden meaning, offering a more profound level of truth, and discernible through a more rational interpretation of the text, is addressed to the chosen few who are equipped to receive it. As Maimonides put it, Scriptural language is cast in metaphors "in order that the uneducated may comprehend it according to the measure of their faculties and the feebleness of their apprehension, while educated persons may take it in a different sense."

The literal reading of the Biblical text would often bypass many invaluable doctrines of our faith. Frequently, moreover, it would even lead us to absurd errors. Thus we have noted that the Torah speaks of God in anthropomorphic terms. It asserts that man is made in the divine image. It describes God as speaking to the prophets, or as walking, seeing, working, resting, sitting, writing, hearing. Taken literally these assertions would involve us in the blasphemy of conceiving God as corporeal and finite. The Torah likewise includes many literary exaggerations which seem fantastic and clearly impossible unless we take them as figures of speech.

The Torah similarly attributes emotions to God. It describes Him as being pleased with the righteous and indignant with the wicked. Emotions describe changes which transpire in an essence and they are clearly inapplicable to God Who is not subject to change. These expressions, too, we have seen, are employed for pedagogic reasons. They concretize the qualities of divine providence, which manifests itself in the universal law of retribution, thereby to create incentives for obedience to the laws of righteousness. Acts of reward and punishments when performed by human beings are associated with certain emotions, and metaphorically these emotions are ascribed to God. "Whenever any of His actions is perceived by us, we ascribe to God that emotion which is the source of the act when performed by ourselves, and call Him by an epithet which is formed of the verb expressing the emotion."

And the same applies to various allegories, literary exaggerations or hyperbolic statements in prophetic literature. "Thus nobody doubts that the blessing 'May the Lord open to thee His good treasures, the Heavens' must be taken figuratively; for God has no treasure in which He keeps the rain. The same is the case with the following passage. . . . 'He opened the doors of Heaven, He rained upon them manna to eat' (Ps. 78:23, 24). No person assumes that there is a door or a gate to heaven, but everyone understands that this is a simile and a figurative expression. In the same way must be understood the following passage. . . . 'Thy heavens were opened' (Ezekiel 1:1); 'If not, blot me out from Thy book which Thou hast written' (Ex. 32:32); 'I will blot him out from the book of life' (ibid, 33). All these phrases are figurative; and we must not assume that God has a book in which

He writes, or from which He blots out, as those generally believe who do not find figurative speech in these passages."

There is another peculiarity in the idiom of prophetic writings which a rational interpretation of the text will clarify, and that is the tendency of the prophets to trace the cause for all events to God. This notion seems in conflict with our experience which shows events as transpiring through more direct causes, whether these causes consist in "substances, physical properties, free will, or chance . . . by free will, I mean that of man . . . or even in the will of another living being." But there is no real conflict. The prophets simply omit the intermediate causes and reckon with the ultimate Cause, Who is the cause behind all intermediate causes. Since God is the source of all intermediate causation, "it can consequently be said that everything which is produced by any of these causes, that God commanded that it should be made, or said that it should be so . . ."

Many people took Scriptural expressions literally, identifying religion with doctrines that were intellectually untenable. It was above all to the emancipation of Scripture from this literalism that Maimonides dedicated his *Guide*: "This work seeks to explain certain obscure figures which occur in the prophets and are not distinctly characterized as being figures. Ignorant and superficial readers take them in a literal, not in a figurative sense. Even well-informed persons are bewildered if they understand these passages in their literal signification, but they are entirely relieved of their perplexity when we explain the figure, or merely suggest that the terms are figurative. For this reason I have called this book *Guide to the Perplexed*."

On the basis of what we may call the rational interpretation of the Bible, Maimonides read many of the specific teachings of Aristotle into the Biblical text. The Aristotelian doctrine of the Intelligences he saw as identical with the Torah's teaching concerning angels. The Aristotelian characterization of the Intelligences parallels fully the characterization of angels in Scriptural and rabbinic sources. And he therefore felt justified in concluding:

"When we assert that Scripture teaches that God rules the world through angels, we mean such angels as are identical with Intelligences."

Various other doctrines in the Aristotelian system were to be found in Scripture, according to Maimonides. The creation account in Genesis and Ezekiel's visions of God, interpreted in a symbolic and allegorical meaning, as intended, offer us respectively all the vital teachings in natural science and metaphysics. These teachings were not stated explicitly because they were judged beyond the intellectual powers of the common people.

A person trained in philosophy knows the necessity of probing deeply into all things in order to attain truth, and he must do the same probing into the Torah. Its superficial reading may repel him, but reaching below the surface, he will discover a mine of precious truth. In the words of Maimonides: "Employ your reason, and you will be able to discern what is said allegorically, figuratively, or hyperbolically, and what is meant literally, exactly according to the original meaning of the words. You will then understand all prophecies, learn and retain rational principles of faith, pleasing in the eyes of God Who is most pleased with truth, and most displeased with falsehood; your mind and heart will not be so perplexed as to believe or accept as law what is untrue or improbable, whilst the Law is perfectly true when properly understood . . ."[14]

The Place of Reason in Religion

We must now consider the defense of Maimonides against the adversary at home—the spokesmen of conventional piety who objected to his entire labor of seeking a rationale for the Torah. For them it was enough that the Torah has spoken. Embodying as it does God's will, its provisions need no other justification. It is God's will rather than any discernible reasons underlying them, that makes them authorative. The entire labor of philosophy was for them a needless excursion into a hostile world. And supporting their view, there were various passages in the Bible and especially in the Talmud, which clearly proscribe religious speculation, as injurious to one's religious faith. These men were akin in their thinking to the Moslem theologians, the Mutakalemim, who saw in the universe only a divine will, for whom events in nature were devoid of any inherent principles of order or rationality, revealing only the majesty, the power and the inscrutible will of God.

For Maimonides, the universe revealed not only the will but also the wisdom of God, and permeating all events were elements of inherent rationality. The discernible rationality of all things was their purposefulness. All things in nature were useful for some end. The Torah, the choicest of God's works, could therefore not be otherwise. It must surely be a work aiming at specific objectives, discernible to the human mind upon careful analysis of its provisions.

Maimonides denied that traditional Judaism was unfriendly to the life of reason. The passages which disparage speculation in religion do not really mean "to close the gates of investigation entirely, and to prevent the mind from comprehending what is within its reach." They are directed against possible abuses in the pursuit of such studies. They are directed against people entering speculative pursuits without being adequately prepared for them.

They are likewise directed against preoccupations with questions which are outside the competence of reason to deal with. Certain questions will always elude us. We cannot know the nature of the planetary worlds; or why God created the universe at a particular time rather than at another; or why He chose to give existence the specific form which He chose to give it; or what the nature is of the "action" by which God sustains the universe; or what is the divine "essence." All we can know is the empirical world. God gave man "power to know the things which are under the heavens; here is man's world, here is his home, into which he has been placed, and of which he is himself a portion. It is in fact ignorance or a kind of madness to weary our minds with finding out things which are beyond our reach. We must content ourselves with that which is within our reach."

It is not only pointless to delve into matters which in the nature of things are outside the reach of our reason. It is bound to produce confusion and doubt and to deflect us from our true course. As the eye will be weakened in the perception of normal phenomena after it has wearied itself with attempting to see what is outside the range of its normal vision, so will the mind. "If a person studies too much and exhausts his reflective powers, he will be confused, and will not be able to comprehend even that which had been within the power of his apprehension." Within the areas of its competence, on the other hand, the pursuit of reason is highly desirable.

Maimonides recognized that there might be conflict between individual statements in traditional religious sources and the current findings of science. If these be matters which touch on the physical universe, then it is the findings of science which should prevail; and our saying so involves no disloyalty to tradition. Such statements, even if made by the most revered of ancient masters, do not reflect prophetic inspiration, which must be adopted. They reflect the cultural background of those masters or their own intellectual labors; and they have no more validity than was inherent in current knowledge or in the rigor of their thinking. Thus we must "not expect that everything our sages say respecting astronomical matters should agree with observation; for mathematics was not fully developed in those days; and their statements were not based on the authority of the prophets, but on the knowledge which they themselves possessed or derived from contemporary men of science."

The prophet's distinctive competence enables him to speak with authority on matters where, in the nature of things, proof is impossible. But where proof is possible, even the prophet is bound by that proof. He cannot negate what rational demonstration establishes unequivocally. Thus, because they clashed with the dictates of reason, Maimonides rejected such popular beliefs of his day as astrology, demonology and various practices of magic. He was undaunted by the fact that some of these beliefs were shared by the highest authorities in the Talmud. "In matters of a speculative nature," he declared, "everyone acts according to the results of his own study and accepts that which appears to him established by proof."[15]

Maimonides was eager to show that in his acknowledgment of a wide area of authority for reason in religion he was not really an innovator, that he was not really bringing an alien element into his faith. He pointed to a Talmudic admission that on some problems in astronomy the pagan thinkers had shown greater accuracy than the sages of Israel, who thereupon "abandoned their own theory in favor of the theory of others." We have already seen his reading into the Biblical text of many of the doctrines of Aristotle. He identified the Aristotelian Intelligences with angels; in the creation account of Genesis he found veiled references to a vast body of teachings in natural science; in the vision of God described in *Ezekiel* he found an elaborate body of teachings in metaphysics.

He likewise found support for his views concerning the metaphoric character of Scriptural anthropomorphisms. He pointed to the well-known rabbinic statement: "The Torah speaks the language of man." There is a Midrash (Bereshit Rabbah ch. 27) which stated this truth even more explicitly. Commenting on Ezekiel's portrayal of God in the image of a man (ch. 1:26), the Midrash asserts: "Great was the power of the prophets; they compared the creature to its Creator." "Our sages have thus stated in plain terms that they are far from believing in the corporeality of God; and in the figures and forms seen in a prophetic vision, though belonging to created beings, the prophets, to use the words of our sages 'compared the creature to its creator'." Thus we have a clear recognition that in their anthropomorphisms the prophets spoke of God by means of analogies borrowed from human experience, a device intended to make God more comprehensible to the common man.[16]

Maimonides felt called on to explain the paucity of philosophic materials in traditional Jewish literature. In part, he suggested, this was due to the fact that such studies were not carried on publicly. They were confined to the select few who had the necessary prerequisite education, and they transmitted their findings orally, without reducing them to writing. Moreover, the conditions of living under foreign domination produced a cultural decadence among Jews, with the result that such studies were neglected and what had been achieved in the past was gradually forgotten.

It was this cultural decadence, too, which produced the widespread distrust of reason in contemporary Judaism. Living among people whose religion is hostile to reason, Jews tended to do likewise, forgetting that this is a departure from the authentic character of Jewish tradition. "We are mixed up with other nations; we have learnt their opinions, and followed their ways and acts. . . . Having been brought up among persons untrained in philosophy, we are inclined to consider these philosophical opinions as foreign to our religion, just as uneducated persons find them foreign to their own notions. But, in fact, it is not so."[17]

The People of Revelation

The Torah embodies all the truth, speculative as well as practical, which mankind needs to attain the highest goals of human life. The Torah arose within the Jewish community, but its goal and scope are universal. It seeks the perfection of all men. What then is the significance of a distinctive Jewish existence in the world? What is the reason for a particular religious community maintaining its own life, apart from the rest of mankind? The Jewish people, Maimonides replied, in the spirit of the traditional conception of Israel, has been selected to be the protagonist of the Torah, to foster its teachings among all mankind. God in an act of free initiative, pursuing designs and purposes in accordance with His own will and wisdom, has singled out Israel for this task, and it is the performance of this task which constitutes their reason to be as a separate, a distinctive community in civilization.

Israel's vocation is the legacy of its patriarchal past. The origins of it go back to the work of Abraham. Raised in an atmosphere of idolatry and superstition, he was the first to rebel against it.

By contemplating the world about him, he came to the vision of one universal God as the source of all the creative energies in the universe. And he dedicated his life to the dissemination of his great spiritual discovery. He made many converts to his faith, but he soon passed away. However his work was continued by those who came after him. And finally his descendants grew into a great people who took up the torch of his faith. It thus became the function of the Jewish people to implement the vision projected by Abraham, the emancipation of mankind from superstition and falsehood through the dissemination of the belief in the unity of God, with its related doctrines. The Jews were under a constant mandate to "invite all mankind to His worship and to faith in Him."

The forms of Jewish group life were for Maimonides important only insofar as they served the higher purpose of their religious vocation. Thus he saw no particular merit in literary expressions in Hebrew, unless the ideas expressed were of an exalted character. Language was only a form; and literary creations "regardless of the language in which they were written, must be appraised in terms of their contents. . . ." He took this stand in opposition to the Hebraists of his day who made language an end in itself. To cite his own revealing explanation: "I have seen elders and pious men of our faith when they are at a festive gathering . . . and someone should desire to sing a song in Arabic, they will object and regard it improper to hear him though the theme of the song be the praise of God or of virtuous living. . . . On the other hand, if a Hebrew song should be chosen, they will not object and it will not disturb them though the text of the song include objectionable or indecent ideas. This is sheer nonsense . . . for it should all depend on the contents. If the theme be exalted it should be encouraged regardless of the language it is in, but if the theme be ignoble, in any language, it should be objected to." Indeed, the very sanctity of Hebrew as the language of the Torah should confine it to a lofty usage and a composition offensive to high moral sensitivity is far more objectionable in Hebrew than in any other language.

The Repudiation of Racialism

Affiliation with Israel, Maimonides explained, was not an accident of blood; it was a matter of conforming to a way of life. Jews were never to impose their religion on others against their will. A Jewish society was to offer free domicile to members of other faiths, as long as they conformed to the universal principles of religion and morality, as summarized in the Torah's seven "Noahite laws." But the voluntary convert whose motives were sincere and honorable was to receive a ready welcome. He was to be accorded a great love and shown due appreciation for his fortitude and faith in coming to cleave to the Jewish people. To the proselyte Obadiah, who had inquired whether it was appropriate for him to pray in the words of the classic liturgy which includes such phrases as "God of *our fathers,*" "Who sanctified *us* with Thy commandments and commanded *us,*" "Who brought *us* out of the land of Egypt," he replied: "Exactly as the man born an Israelite prays, so do you likewise, whether you pray in private or whether you conduct a service in public. . . . It was our father Abraham who taught all people and informed them of the true religion and the unity of God, spurned idolatry and overthrew its worship, brought many under the wings of the Shekinah and cultivated them and instructed them. Therefore every one who becomes a convert until the end of all generations, and everyone who acknowledges the unity of God as it is written in the Torah, is a disciple of our father Abraham and a member of his household. . . . Let not your descent be lightly esteemed in your eyes. If we trace our geneological tree to Abraham, Isaac and Jacob, you may trace yours to the Creator of the Universe."

The truth, moreover, Maimonides made it clear, is not an exclusive possession of Israel. Individuals in other communities may come upon it, and their worth is in no way diminished because they remain outside the fold of Israel. All noble human beings, of any nation, have, he declared in his code, the same sanctity as priests and Levites in Israel. The latter derive their privileged position in Jewish society from the fact that they were teachers of virtue and truth. And any one whose life is dedicated to a similar service enjoys the very same high worth.

To a correspondent he explained in similar vein: "And there is no doubt about the matter that whoever corrects his soul with purity of morals and purity of knowledge in the faith of the Creator will assuredly be of the children of the world to come. For this reason our Rabbis stated. 'Even a pagan who occupies himself with the Torah of Moses is equal in worth to a High Priest in Israel'." The patriarchs, Noah and Adam, never observed the rituals of the Torah, but that did not make them ignoble people. These rituals are purely instrumental; they aim to enlighten and to ennoble, to broaden our knowledge of God, and to improve the quality of our conduct. And one who achieves these virtues through another channel is a man of God, to be reckoned with the noblest of Israel.

On Christianity and Islam

There is very little direct religious polemics in his writings, but Maimonides was gravely critical of Islam and Christianity. He resented their claims to have displaced Israel as the vehicle of the divine revelation in history, their nullification of Biblical law, their repudiation of the primacy of the Mosaic tradition. He alluded to Mohammed's sensuality, a glaring character deficiency in one posing as a prophet. In the case of Christianity he also objected to the doctrine of the trinity as a compromise of true monotheism. While the persistant evil in the world reminded him that the Messianic age, however it might be defined, was in some far off future; the Messiah had not yet appeared.

Nevertheless he paid tribute to both Mohammedanism and Christianity for the great strides toward the truth made by mankind under their influences. Of the Moslems he wrote: "They are in no way idolators, and idol-worship has long since passed from their mouths and hearts. They ascribe unity to God as is proper, a unity without blemish . . ." Even the devotions around the

Kaabeh or "black stone" in Mecca, a survival of an older idolatry, did not deter Maimonides from this judgment, for the rites had been reinterpreted and redirected to the worship of the true God.

The attitude of the Christians in his day toward images and icons seemed to Maimonides idolatrous but he saw Christianity too in sympathetic terms. He encouraged one of his correspondents to help Christians with the study of the Torah, remarking: "They acknowledge that our Torah was given to us from God by our teacher Moses . . . and they regard it in its entirety as Holy Scriptures, though at times they interpret it wrongly."

Despite their misinterpretations of many fundamental doctrines of the Holy Scripture, God in His mysterious wisdom has used these two faiths as aids in the moral and religious regeneration of the world. For through them "the entire world has been filled with the doctrines of the Messiah, the Torah and the commandments. These doctrines have been propagated to the distant isles and among many peoples, uncircumcised of heart and flesh." These faiths will, in the perspective of history, prove to have been "the trail blazers" for the true Messianic fulfillment that yet awaits mankind.

The Martyrdom of Israel

The high calling for which God had selected Israel was not without its price. The world seldom honors the carrier of new truths, who would disturb the conventional faith and life. And incidental to the performance of their vocation in history, the Jews, though serving mightily the cause of human progress, were to expect misunderstanding and ill-will. Maimonides himself had tasted that ill-will in full measure. At the age of 13, he was forced to flee his native Spain, in the wake of anti-Jewish persecutions under the Almohades, a fanatical Moslem sect who came into possession of the country, and it took him several years of wandering before he and his family finally settled in friendlier Egypt.

Maimonides regarded those disabilities of Jewish life as the resistance of the world to the challenge of Judaism. He counselled his people wherever possible to migrate to countries that accord their citizens religious liberty. He was sympathetic with the "marranos," those who, to escape death, pretended conversion to the dominant faith. Indeed, when faced with the emergency, he counselled appeasing the Moslem fanatics with the verbal acknowledgment of Mohammed as Allah's true prophet, rather than submitting to martyrdom in refusing. Life was too precious and not to be jeopardized when a temporary minor compromise would save it. But above all he called upon them to face their fate with fortitude and trust, and to cling all the more zealously to the teachings of their religion. Human hands will not undo the divine purpose. History demonstrates that the triumphs of tyranny are short-lived. In the end, Israel will outlive its persecutors. And by their very courage and steadfastness under attack, they will win new admiration from the world, and make new gains for their cause.

Toward National Rebirth

Maimonides held that Israel's performance of its vocation in history was impaired as a result of living in the diaspora. Constant persecutions have caused a physical and intellectual deterioration in Jewry. Being insecure, the Jews could not give themselves, with any degree of concentration, to intellectual pursuits. The diaspora, moreover, had made impossible a centralized leadership in world Judaism. The full rabbinic ordination, and an authoritative Sanhedrin to exercise supreme authority in Judaism, are possible only in Palestine. Without these institutions, Jewish life is incomplete, and cannot adequately play its role in the world.

The circumstances of living in the diaspora have likewise robbed Israel of prophecy. Prophets cannot do their work in a society that is disjointed, scattered, and without the attribute of autonomy. "Our sages say, inspiration does not come upon a prophet when he is sad or languid. . . . The same circumstances, prevalence of sadness and dullness, were undoubtedly the direct cause of the interruption of prophecy during the exile. Such an evil state has been prophesied to us in the words (Amos 8:12, Lam. 2:9) 'They shall turn to and fro to seek the word of God, but shall not find it'; 'Her King and her princes are among the nations, the law is no more, her prophets also find no vision from the Lord.' This is a real fact, and the cause is evident; the prerequisites (of prophecy) have been lost. In the Messianic period—may it soon commence, prophecy will therefore again be in our midst, as has been promised by God."

The diaspora will not remain a permanent condition of Jewish existence, Maimonides assured his people. In the fullness of time, there will be a Jewish restoration in Palestine. Israel will be reborn as a free people on its ancestral soil. The adventure of the Jewish creative spirit in action will be resumed, after a fateful lapse through many centuries. The day of final liberation will, however, embrace all mankind within its beneficence. The freedom of the Jewish people will be a phase of the larger freedom which will dawn for all men throughout the world.

The term by which the period of the restoration is known in tradition is the "Messianic age." It was so called because it was to be inaugurated under the leadership of "the anointed one," in Hebrew, the *Messiah,* a reference to the ceremony of anointment with oil, by which Jewish kings were customarily inducted to their office. The Messiah was to be a leader of ideal stature, a ruler and prophet, combining within himself courage, wisdom, a great passion for righteousness, and skill in the arts of war. Maimonides attached great importance to the martial qualities of the Messiah. He was aware that great transformations in the world frequently evoke fierce resistance, and a world liberator must know how to lead his hosts against the powers of evil opposing his cause. It is significant, too, that Maimonides ascribed the fall of the Jewish state to the Jewish neglect of their armed forces. Physical force cannot be resisted with moral power alone, and those who champion justice must also have force on their side if they are to win in battle and assure their survival in the world.

The Messianic redemption, according to Maimonides, was to be inaugurated without any play of miracles. In popular religion, the Messiah was pictured as a miracle-worker, while the new world order was to be a supernaturally transformed plane of existence sharply different from the world as we now know it. Maimonides denied this. The new order, according to him, was to be achieved through the brilliant leadership of the Messiah himself. And that new order was to be a continuation of our present world, changed only through the elimination of the strife of men and nations, and the removal of human oppression which is today ravaging the world.

The resolution of conflicts and tensions will be the crowning achievement of the Messiah who will thus bring peace to the world. And when Israel is restored as a free people in Palestine, it will likewise be dedicated to peaceful ends, to the service of God and man, and not to self-aggrandizement as a nation. Despite painful memories of humiliation and betrayal, Israel will know no rancor or will to revenge. "The sages and the prophets did not long for the days of the Messiah for the purpose of wielding dominion over all the world, or of ruling over the heathens, or being exalted by the peoples." Their principal desire was for the freedom to concentrate on the study and practice of the Torah and the pursuit of the intellectual life.

Israel, in other words, will utilize her new freedom for a renewal of spiritual creativity for its own and for universal human blessing. And that will mark the dawn of history's great consummation. "In that era, there will not be famine or war, jealousy or strife. The sole occupation throughout the world will be to know the Lord. As it is said (Is. 11:9) 'And the earth shall be full of the knowledge of the Lord as the waters cover the sea'."[18]

The paths of Israel and of the nations will at last have converged, and the point of convergence will be universal fulfillment, universal acknowledgment of God, and universal understanding and peace among men.

Chapter V

MAN AS A CITIZEN OF THE UNIVERSE

Man's place in the universe and the significance of his life on earth was another of the great issues which challenged thinking men at the time of Maimonides. The traditional doctrine of man was clear. It was a grand conception. It made man the center of the universe, the end for which all else in creation was formed. Man enjoyed moral freedom; he was undetermined in his will to choose one course of action or another. He was sovereign over his life, and he could mold his character freely, in the image of his own conception of the good. Human life, moreover, was surrounded by the special providence of God, who cared for every individual person, meting out the rewards of each man in accordance with his merits.

The traditional doctrine of man was challenged by the current teachings of philosophy. The prevailing view of the philosophers was that the universe had not been created, that it was an eternal process which had gone on without beginning and which would go on indefinitely, without end. An eternal universe cannot possibly have any final cause for its existence, and man cannot therefore be the center of the universe. For man existed simultaneously with all else in existence. Everything is part of one enterprise which we can only describe, but which we must accept as a final fact, whose ultimate reason for being cannot be questioned.

The belief in man's free will likewise came under challenge. The popular "science" of astrology taught that man's life was determined by the stars. Man could do nothing below that was not ordained for him by the configuration of the stars above. Man's free will was likewise denied by certain theologians. Impressed with the conception of God's sovereignty and might, they could not grant man the freedom to do as he pleased. Man's free-

72

dom would in a sense limit God's freedom, His all pervading power to govern the universe. They therefore developed the idea that God determines man's life, that whatever man was at any given time, he was simply what God then caused him to be.

Current thought also challenged the traditional doctrine of man in its denial of divine providence. The Aristotelians believed in divine providence, but they interpreted it in naturalistic terms. They meant by it that an influence emanated from God which gave direction and movement to all things in the universe. This applied however only to the species of each element in existence. It applied for instance to humanity as a whole, to the universal species, *man*. The particular individuals which comprise each species, who are born and perish and who are only accidental variations of a common, universal essence—they held to be governed by chance. As an argument for their belief, they cited a technical point about the nature of knowledge. A universal essence can be known by reason. The particular individuals, on the other hand, are known only by the senses. Obviously the only kind of knowledge we may possibly ascribe to God is the knowledge of reason; sense knowledge cannot be ascribed to Him at all. And since God cannot take cognizance of particular individuals, He cannot possibly provide for them. Thus they consigned the individual person to the ravages of chance, to the mercy of shifting circumstances, without the beneficent concern of God as to any significant realization in his life.

Perhaps more telling was the argument they cited from the phenomenon of evil in the world. If God concerned Himself with the destinies of individuals, there would be evidence of it in the empirical facts of human existence; there would be a discernible order in the affairs of mankind. The facts, as they read them, belie such order. As we gauge the careers of people we find indiscriminant suffering, we find frustration and defeat, often endured by the noblest of men, while the wicked frequently prosper and live out their lives in dignity and peace. If God really cared about people, as individuals, He would not allow all this to go on unchecked in the world.

Man Not the Center of the Universe

Maimonides did not believe in the eternity of the universe. Yet he joined the spokesmen of current philosophy in denying man's central position in the universe. He too, believed that the universe is without any discernible "final cause," even though he held firmly to the conviction that the universe had been created in time. God undoubtedly had His reasons for launching existence, when He did, and as He did. But that is not something that man can discern. We cannot therefore identify the human person as the one element in universal existence to say that he was the ulti- mate reason for God's act of cosmic creation. We cannot know why the Lord brought existence into being, except to say that His will, His wisdom so prompted it. If it were possible to identify any one creature in the universe and say that existence came into being because of him, we would be defining God's ultimate pur- poses. These, in truth, elude us.

Maimonides thus rejected what was a common belief in popu- lar religion—that the universe exists for man's sake. Man, Mai- monides conceded readily, is the most perfect being on earth, but in the face of the vast planetary realms, the celestial beings above, man is an inferior and lowly creature. Indeed, man's abode itself, the earth, is only an insignificant unit in the planetary system. A creature of earth cannot therefore presume to pose as the most important being in the universe, and surely not the reason for its existence.

Indeed, we may not look upon man as the final cause of even all earthly things. Many objects in nature clearly function to meet human needs, but that is not necessarily the ultimate reason for their existence. For man could have been created differently than he is now, without depending on the objects that now serve to sustain his life. Man cannot therefore be considered as their only reason for existence. Man is not inherently dependent on them, and if they had no other purpose, they would really be a vain creation. The notion that man is the final cause of all other existent things, is necessarily associated with the belief that the universe is created, but believing in creation, "we must admit that God could have created the universe in a different manner as regards the causes and effects contained in it, and this would lead to the absurd conclusion that everything except man existed without any purpose, as the principal object, man, could have been brought into existence without the rest of the creation."

Apart from the will of God, we cannot ultimately account for the universe, whether all of it or any part of it. We may thus regard all things as ends in themselves; they were all brought into being by the same act of God's will. Maimonides concludes the discussion of this theme with the following position, which he offers "as most correct according to the teaching of the Bible, and best in accordance with the results of philosophy": "the universe does not exist for man's sake, but each being exists for its own sake, and not because of some other being."

Maimonides defended his doctrine as not really a deviation from the essential teachings of his religious tradition, popular notions to the contrary notwithstanding. He cited many passages in the traditional texts in support of his view. Thus the Day of Atonement liturgy includes the following: "Thou hast distinguished man from the beginning, and chosen him to stand before Thee; who can say unto Thee what doest Thou? And if he be righteous, what does he give Thee?" This passage, as Maimonides saw it, clearly implies that the ultimate final cause of existence is unknowable, "that it was not a final cause that determined the existence of all things but only His will." Another passage, Proverbs 16:4, seemed to offer more explicit support for his views. It asserts: "The Lord has made everything *lemanehu*" (for its or His purpose). If we render *lemanehu* as "for its purpose," then we have a specific affirmation of the view that all things have been created for themselves, and not as means to another end. If we render *lemanehu* as "for His purpose" then we have a declaration that things exist because God so willed it, again omitting every reference to a final cause responsible for their creation. Through these and other citations Maimonides offered traditional backing for his view which denies man the conventionally ascribed role as the final cause of the universe. He is not even the final cause of the sublunary world which is his home, though he is obviously its most distinguished citizen.[1]

Frontiers of Human Freedom

Maimonides rejected every attempt to compromise man's free will. God is master of the universe, but He does not predestine man on birth as to the moral quality of his life. "Let not your mind entertain the assertion of the fools of other peoples and also of the many uninformed men among the Israelites that the Holy One blessed be He, decrees concerning the human being from his birth, whether he is to be righteous or wicked; the matter is not so. There is no one to compel, decree, or determine him as to either of the two ways; but it is he, of his own accord and mind, who inclines toward whichever way he prefers."

Man's freedom is circumscribed only by hereditary limitations with which he is born. But these merely define the extremities of possible development. Within those extremities there is ample room for free action. And what man really becomes depends generally on how he exercises his freedom, rather than on the quality of his constitutional endowments. Thus, "if one who inclines constitutionally toward a certain excellence is left entirely without instruction, and if his faculties are not stimulated, he will undoubtedly remain ignorant. On the other hand, if one, by nature dull and phlegmatic . . . is instructed and enlightened, he will, though with difficulty, it is true, gradually succeed in acquiring knowledge and understanding."

Man is also influenced by his environment. The way of life of his society impinges upon him and he feels greatly constrained to adapt himself and conform to it. But this is not a determining influence. For man can choose his environment. He can migrate to other countries that will be more hospitable to his way of life, or he can court the unpopularity of men and withdraw from their fellowship, though remaining physically in their midst. In any case the ultimate decision as to the quality of man's life rests with himself; it is not imposed from without. The restraining agency of his life is "in his very self, I mean in his human framework. When the latter becomes perfected it is exactly that which keeps him away from those things . . . which are termed vices; and it is that which spurs him on to . . . virtue."

Maimonides was particularly emphatic in denouncing the popular notions of astral determinism. "Thou mayest not believe the absurd ideas of astrologers," he wrote, "who falsely assert that the constellation at the time of ones birth, determines whether one is to be virtuous or vicious, the individual being thus necessarily compelled to follow out a certain line of conduct." Such beliefs are no more than superstitions and should be shunned as such. The whole subject of astrology, he advised a community that sought guidance from him on the subject, is "not science at all but folly. . . . Nobody adheres to it except a simpleton who believes anything or the person who wishes to deceive others."

If man's conduct were determined, reasoned Maimonides, it would cease to have moral quality. Man would be beyond good and evil and there would be no such thing as a moral order, which implies free will in human decisions. For "if God were to decree concerning man whether he is to be righteous or wicked, or if there were anything in the nature of his nativity which impelled him to either of the two ways . . . as the foolish astrologers invent in their minds, how could He have commanded us through the prophets to do this and avoid that. . . .? What place would there have been for the whole of the Torah? And by what justice or by what right, could He punish the wicked or reward the righteous?"

There were some who regarded the doctrine of man's free will as inconsistent with the principle of divine government in the universe. For, if events represent the unfolding of a divine plan, then God has a knowledge of events before they transpire. Were a person to behave differently than he actually does, he would presumably come in conflict with the divine plan. Indeed, if a person were completely free to use his own discretion as to vital decisions in his life, we would have to concede a large realm of existence in which the divine government does not operate.

Maimonides disposes of these objections as based on a false conception of what the divine government of the world is. The root of the error in these objections is their presupposition "that God's knowledge is like ours." Actually God's knowledge is unique and wholly different from human knowledge. Since the nature of God's knowledge is unknown, we cannot regard it as inconsistent with another article of our faith, freedom of will. Considering the dictum of tradition on the subject, Maimonides adds, we may surely assert that whatever God's knowledge ultimately is, it is not in itself a causal force. "The fact that God knows things while in a state of possibility, when their existence belongs to the future, does not change the nature of the possible in any way; that nature remains unchanged; and the knowledge of the realization of one of several possibilities does not yet effect the realization. God's knowledge of one of the eventualities does not determine it, however certain that knowledge may be concerning the future occurence of the one eventuality."

As to the assertion that human freedom leaves a realm of existence which is beyond the divine government, it is likewise untrue. For that itself is divinely ordained, that there should be human freedom. "Just as God willed that man should be upright in stature, broadchested and have fingers, likewise did He will that man should move or rest of his own accord, and that his actions should be such as his own free will dictates to him, without any undue influence or restraint."

Human freedom is limited by the pattern of life itself. Man's behaviour becomes habituated and it is difficult for him freely to alter his conduct in ready response to the dictates of reason. However, even after our behaviour pattern is established, we need not become permanently attached to it. For difficult though it admittedly is, man can reconstruct his pattern of living in consonance with new convictions.

Maimonides called such reconstructions a soul "cure," for he regarded any character propensity which is a distortion of the ideal as a spiritual illness. Such "cure" consists in a drastic departure from the habit one wishes to break and a changing over to its extreme opposite. Through constant repetition of this line of action, the fixed pattern will finally be broken and then a new equilibrium will be established, leading to a more acceptable way of life. The man who suffers from niggardliness, for instance, must be taught to squander, "till that propensity which was the cause of his avarice has totally disappeared. Then when he reaches that point when he is about to become a squanderer, we must teach him to moderate his profusion. . . . If, on the other hand, a man is a squanderer, he must be directed to practice strict economy, and to repeat acts of niggardliness. It is not necessary, however, for him to perform acts of avarice as many times as mean men should those of profusion. . . . The mean man needs to practice lavishness to a greater degree than should be required of the lavish to practice meanness. This is a fundamental principle of the science of curing moral ills, and is worthy of remembrance."

The reconstruction of our behaviour patterns is illustrated in the discipline of repentance which is fundamental to the religious life. There could be no repentance if we were wholly determined by our past. In other words, the possibility of repentance implies man's supremacy over his behaviour pattern. The power of habit conditions our freedom, but habit itself will yield to rethinking and reconstruction. It was the recognition of this truth which led Maimonides to treat the subject of free will as a phase of the general theme of repentance.[2]

Divine Providence and the Problem of Evil

Maimonides also defended the traditional doctrine that God's providence extends to individuals. He denied the validity of the argument from knowledge offered by the philosophers. It had been their argument that God cannot provide for individuals because

He does not know particulars. God's knowledge can apply only to universals, to ultimate essences of things, or the species of each type of existence. But this argument is based on the assumption that we can characterize God's knowledge from what we know of human knowledge. This is not so. God's knowledge is the knowledge of the Creator Who knows the whole because it is the offspring of His design. Even the emergent future is known to Him without involving a change in His knowledge since that future too is part of His unfolding plan. Our knowledge, on the other hand, is synthetic, and from the outside. It has to be shaped through each particular experience, and it is never complete, never whole. How can two such types of knowledge be compared or analogies drawn between them? As for the argument that the knowledge of particulars is a sensate knowledge which we may not ascribe to God—it may apply to creatures other than man. And here Maimonides admitted that providence extended only to the species and not to individuals. But this does not apply in the case of individual humans. For God has seen fit to impart of His reason to individual human beings. That is indeed their distinctive excellence in creation. And God's knowledge and providence reaches human individuals to the extent that their reason has been actively developed. Sensate knowledge is thus not involved here at all.

Maimonides was fully aware of the presence of evil in the world. He had himself tasted it in full measure. But he denied that evil, as we experience it in the world, was really inconsistent with a divine government over human lives. He pleaded first for setting the problem in proper relation to the facts. Some people exaggerated the facts and drew up an indictment of the universe wholly out of proportion to the realities in the case. There was an Arab theologian Al-Razi who even tabulated statistics on the pains and joys of life, and came to the conclusion that "there exists more evil than good," and that creation is a failure. Such theorizing is generally born of a blindness to the affirmative aspects of life. We take for granted the vast areas of order and beauty and goodness and lift the isolated evil to make of it the perspective by which to judge the whole vast enterprise of existence. Our problem is real enough, but it must be approached with a sense of proportion.

There are three essential categories of evil to which human life is exposed. There is the evil which we suffer by virtue of our being bodily creatures, subject to the accidents of time and space. This includes our various illnesses, natural deformities, and death itself. "It is on account of the body that some persons happen to have great deformities or paralysis of some of the organs. This evil may be part of the natural constitution of those persons, or may have developed subsequently in consequence of changes in the elements such as through bad air, or thunderstorms, or landslips." There are the evils which we bring upon one another in various acts of cruelty, of injustice, and war. And there are the evils of which we suffer most frequently—those we bring upon ourselves, primarily through the quest for the superfluous things of life. "This class of evil originates in man's vices, such as the excessive desire for eating, drinking, and love; indulgence in those things in undue measure, or in improper manner, or partaking of bad food. This cause brings disease and affliction upon body and soul alike."

The one thing which evils of all categories have in common is their representing areas of non-existence, rather than positive attributes. This is certainly true of the evils we suffer because of our frailties as bodily creatures. Thus blindness is not a positive attribute like vision; it is rather the lack of an attribute, the absence of vision. It is an area of life over which has not passed the creative presence of God.

The man-made evils too, derive ultimately from non-existence, the non-existence of wisdom. "All the great evils which men cause to each other . . . originate in ignorance which is the absence of wisdom. A blind man, for example, who has no guide stumbles constantly, because he cannot see, and brings injury and harm to himself and others. In the same manner various classes of men, each in proportion to his ignorance, bring great evils upon themselves and upon other individual members of the species. If men possessed wisdom, which stands in the same relation as the sight to the eye, they would not cause any injury to themselves or to others; for the knowledge of truth . . . removes hatred and quarrels and prevents mutual injuries."

The greatest source of human grief is the struggle for material things, but whatever is really vital for man's life, God has made readily available to him; and its abundance is in direct measure to our need for it. "The more necessary a thing is for living beings, the more easily it is found and the cheaper it is; the less necessary it is, the rarer and the dearer it is. Thus, air, water and food are indispensable to man; air is most necessary, for if a man is without air a short time he dies; whilst he can be without water a day or two. Air is also undoubtedly found more easily and is cheaper than water. Water is more necessary than food; for some people can be four or five days without food, provided they have water; water also exists in every country in larger quantities than food and is also cheaper. The same proportions can be noticed in the different kinds of food; that which is more necessary in a certain place exists there in larger quantities and is cheaper than that which is less necessary. . . . This shows the kindness of God to His creatures, even to us weak beings."

Only for the superfluous things must men struggle arduously, but those things are really unnecessary for his life. Maimonides portrayed in vivid details the ravages to human happiness caused by the desire for superfluous things. "The soul, when accustomed to superfluous things, acquires a strange habit of desiring things which are neither necessary for the preservation of the individual, nor for that of the species. This desire is without limit. . . . You desire to have vessels of silver, but golden vessels are still better; others have even vessels of sapphire or perhaps they may be made of emeralds or rubies. . . . Those who are ignorant and perverse in their thoughts are constantly in trouble and pain, because they cannot get as much of superfluous things as another person possesses."

Evil, in other words, derives wholly from negations, from the non-existence of certain positive attributes, while the corresponding existences would cancel these evils and constitute a good. God cannot therefore be said to have fashioned evil, for "He only fashions positive existences, and all positive existences are good."

God's only relationship to these evils consists in the fact that He created matter which is the source of all negations. All bodily existences are transitory existences, subject to the ravages of circumstances, and all the evils which bodily creatures suffer, are in consequence of this quality of matter. The drive behind that mischief we bring upon our fellowmen as well as upon ourselves is likewise a derivative of our bodily natures. The "evil impulse" which spurs us on toward this mischief is another of the inherent characteristics of matter.

The evils wrought by matter are, however, only incidental to its positive functioning. For God did not create matter so that it might perform mischief in human life. It is the fact that man, as a bodily creature, is mortal and subject to "genesis and destruction" which makes possible the constant emergence of new life and the progressive perfecting of the human species. "If man were never subject to change there could be no generation; there would be but one single being, and no individuals forming a species." Even the creation of matter with all its qualities that so often spell suffering for man, must thus be regarded as a good, since it is the means of "perpetuating existence and the continuity of individual beings through the emergence of one after the withdrawal of the other."

And God did not doom man to folly and mischief through the evil impulses of matter. For He endowed us with a force to counter-balance the promptings of our bodily natures, our intellects. As we mature in years, our intellects come increasingly into play to order our lives in accordance with reason. In the fullness of time, mankind as a whole will become enlightened and will emancipate itself from the follies and tragedies which now prevail in life. "This state of society" Maimonides explained, "is promised us by the prophet in the words (Isa. 11:6-9): 'And the wolf shall dwell with the lamb,' etc. The prophet also points out what will be the cause of this change; for he says that hatred, quarrels and fighting will come to an end, because men will then have a true knowledge of God: 'They shall not hurt nor destroy in my holy mountain; for the earth shall be full of the knowledge of the Lord as the waters cover the sea'."

The distresses of human life are then a concomitant of our being what we are, bodily creatures, endowed with free will, whose intellects are only a potentiality as life commences, who must mature and grow and develop toward rational living. And once we accept ourselves for what we are, we may not rebel at what follows inevitably from our natures. It would be asking for the self-contradictory to be on the one hand bodily creatures and at the same time, to be free of those consequences which flow necessarily from our bodily natures. Even God does not do the self-contradictory.

The cry against an equitable order in the universe, Maimonides adds, invariably stems from an illusory notion as to man's place in the scheme of creation. It is based on the assumption that man is the center of the cosmos, and that existence has no other purpose but to cater to his needs. But this is not so, as has already been indicated. On earth below man may be the most important creature; but earthly beings do not exhaust the galaxy of God's creation. The cosmos has purposes other than man, and he cannot therefore press with so much insistence that either he be granted all his heart's desires or else there is no equitable order in God's universe.

Man's life, moreover, Maimonides assures us, cannot ultimately be defeated, for he has God to lean on. This is the great truth expounded in the book of Job. Job rebelled against his fate when he was still in ignorance, living by the simple faith of one whose religion had never passed beyond the traditional. Then he assumed that man's highest good is the attainment of the successes most men seek, such as health, wealth and children. This is why he cried out in anguish when he was robbed of these goods. After his enlightenment, he realized that man's highest good is the knowledge of God, and that it cannot be affected by tragedies such as came upon him. The humble resignation to God, the realization that His will, His way with the world, must necessarily elude us, is bound to "lighten every accident, and the accidents will not beget doubts concerning God. . . . And as our sages wrote 'the pious do everything out of love and rejoice in their afflictions'."

The truly pious person, Maimonides finally added, is not at the mercy of the world, even in its present unregenerate state. He has the fortitude to transcend it. In the measure that man achieves fellowship with God, a fellowship rooted in understanding and in love, he has become impregnable to the world. The evils that rage cannot touch him; he is above the accidents of time and space. The world can hurt him only in moments when he withdraws from divine communion. "If man frees his thoughts from worldly matters, obtains a knowledge of God in the right way, and rejoices in that knowledge, it is impossible that any kind of evil shall befall him while he is with God and God with him. When he does not meditate on God, when he is separated from God, then God is also separated from him; for it is only that intellectual link with God that secures the presence of providence and protection from evil accidents."

Such a person can face the twilight of living without terror. For the diminution of bodily strength does not dim our capacities to know and to love God. Indeed, as the turmoil of living dies down, we acquire more of that serenity which aids us in concentrating on the life of the spirit. And thus man can face death itself unafraid. "The more the forces of his body are weakened and the fire of passion quenched, in the same measure does man's intellect increase in strength and light; his knowledge becomes purer and he is happy with his knowledge. When this perfect man is stricken in age and is near death, his knowledge mightily increases, his joy in that knowledge grows greater, and his love for the object of his knowledge more intense, and it is in this great delight that the soul separates from the body. . . ." In the meta-phor of the rabbis, such men die by a kiss of God, which means "in the midst of the pleasure derived from the knowledge of God and their great love for Him."

The supreme reward which awaits the man who has lived with virtue and wisdom is to share in the life of the world to come. It is his eternal existence as spirit, when the bodily veil which separates him from God is withdrawn. As a bodily creature man is mortal; he is "bound to die and become dissolved into his component elements." But his growth of soul, his intellectual potentialities realized render him immortal. For the rational faculty which is the distinctive soul of man is not a bodily substance that it should decompose into its elements. It is a simple divine element, an emanation from God Himself. And when the body perishes, the soul "returns to the original source whence it issued and remains immortal for all eternity." For a person who has cultivated his soul, death thus becomes not the final doom but a prelude to a new and more exalted level of existence.

The classic term for this doctrine of survival in the rabbinic tradition is *tehiyat hametim,* which means resurrection of the dead —a term employed by Maimonides as well. In the popular belief, these immortal souls were accordingly pictured as due for a re-union with their former bodies, which were to be resurrected for a renewed existence. The eternal life of the world to come was thus to be a bodily existence. Maimonides dismissed this as naive. According to him, the resurrected bodies would again die, to leave the soul alone to enjoy immortality. For what could possibly be the function of the body in the world to come, considering that there are no material enjoyments after death? "Behold it has been explained that the entire necessity for the existence of the body is for one function, and that is the reception of food for the preservation of the body, and the propagation of its kind for the preservation of the species. When that function is removed because its necessity no longer exists . . . as our sages have in-formed us, 'In the world to come there is no eating, drinking or sexual intercourse' . . . that is clear evidence of the non-existence of the body. Because God brings nothing into existence to serve no purpose whatever. . . . And if the people of the world to come are not possessed of organs, but are just bodies . . . perhaps solid globes, or pillars or cubes . . . this is simply ludicrous."

Maimonides was aware that for many people the denial of a bodily level of survival would be a crushing disappointment. But he summoned them to another order of being, infinitely richer and more meaningful, than they dare anticipate: "In the world to come there is no bodily form . . . Nor can any of the accidents to which bodies are subject in this world occur there. Perhaps that bliss will be lightly esteemed by you, and you will think that the reward for fulfilling the commandments and for being perfect in the ways of truth consists in nothing else than indulging in fine food and drink, enjoying beautiful women, wearing raiment of fine linen and embroidery, dwelling in apartments of ivory, and using vessels of silver and gold and similar luxuries, as those foolish and ignorant Arabs imagine who are steeped in sensuality. But wise and intelligent men know that all these things are nonsense and vanity and quite futile. . . . As for the great bliss which the soul is to enjoy in the world to come, there is no possibility of comprehending it or knowing it in this world; because in this world we are only cognisant of the welfare of the body and for that we long. But the bliss of the world to come is exceedingly great and cannot bear comparison with the happiness of this world except in a figurative manner. . . ."[3]

The Hierarchy of Values

The phenomenon of evil in the world, as Maimonides analyzed it, is to a great extent a consequence of our own ignorance as to the true wisdom of life. Maimonides was therefore anxious to guide people in the formulation of a pattern of living that would lead them toward a wiser and more noble existence. Man, according to Maimonides, was a bodily creature, a physical being, subject to the necessities of physical existence. Residing in the physical frame, however, was the intellect, which gives form to the body, and guides life toward its highest goals. The good to be sought in life must therefore begin with the needs of the physical dimension of our existence and then rising to the intellectual.

The Physical Basis of Life

The good life begins with meeting the various claims of our physical existence. For no person will be able to enter upon any more significant level of values until he has secured the means by which the natural basis of life may be maintained. "The well-being of the soul comes undoubtedly first in rank, but the other, the well-being of the body . . . is anterior in nature and time. The latter object is required first because the well-being of the soul can only be obtained after that of the body has been secured; for a person that is suffering from great hunger, thirst, heat or cold, cannot grasp an idea even if communicated by others, much less can he arrive at it by means of his own reasoning. But when a person is in possession of the first perfection, then he may possibly acquire the second perfection, which is undoubtedly of a superior kind, and is alone the source of eternal life."

There are various remarks in the writings of Maimonides which disparage the body. He holds it responsible for all the imperfections of human life. "All obstacles which prevent man from attaining his highest aim in life, all the deficiencies in the character of man, all his evil propensities are to be traced to the body alone." This is true only in the sense that man is constantly under the temptation to make bodily life an end in itself, to live for the cultivation of bodily pleasures and for the accumulation of material things. This is evil. "When a man follows his lusts, allows his desires to master his thoughts, and sets aside his intellect for his cravings, until he returns to the level of the beast which formulates no other longing to its soul than eating, drinking, sexual intercourse, then the divine power, i.e., intellect, cannot manifest itself and he becomes a mere creature swimming in the sea of matter."

On the other hand where the body serves as the means to a nobler end, to make possible the cultivation of the intellectual life, then bodily existence itself becomes exalted; it partakes of the worth of the larger end which it serves. A person who directs all his existence to the service of God, serves Him continually, "even at the time when he is engaged in commerce, even when performing his marital duties; because his object in all this is to provide his needs, so that his body may be perfect to serve the Lord. Even at the time when he sleeps . . . provided he sleeps that both his mind and body may enjoy rest, so that he may not become ill and become unable to serve the Lord when he is not well . . . his very sleep will be found to be a service of the Omnipresent, blessed be He."

Because the body is the indispensable means by which the life of reason sustains itself, one is morally committed to safeguard the body and maintain it in a state of health. Indeed, Maimonides included in his code of religious law an elaborate discussion of hygiene and diet. Bodily exercise, taking eight hours sleep nightly, choosing the proper food, regular bathing—these and a host of other details in the regimen of healthy living are ordained as religious imperatives. He prefaced this discussion with the remark: "Since the preservation of the body belongs to the way of life prescribed by God . . . for it is impossible for a man to understand or have any knowledge of the Creator when he is in poor physical condition . . . it is consequently necessary that he should keep himself aloof from things which are injurious to the body and accustom himself to the things which are healthful and invigorating."

The ascetic negations of the claims of the body Maimonides denounced as evil. Asceticism may be adopted temporarily for purposes of moral therapy, as a drastic reaction from a life of self-indulgence, but not as a continuous way of life. Some of the prophets lived ascetic lives, but they were not exemplifying the highest good. Their asceticism was a protest against the pleasure seeking and luxury loving multitudes of their day. By their asceticism they sought to bear witness to other goods, to the values of the life of reason, which were being ignored in contemporary culture. All impulses and drives which human nature manifests, including those we normally associate with bodily life, are God's gifts to man and they are meant for his good. They become evil, when they are given undue place in the pattern of living, when they are allowed too much or too little room for self-expression. Indeed the problem of morals is, in one sense, a quest for the golden mean that will define the exact scope for each natural drive in our make-up. But complete suppression of any phase of our nature is a grievous error.

Maimonides rebuked those who chastise "their bodies with all kinds of afflictions, imagining that they had acquired perfection and moral worth, and that by this means man would approach nearer to God, as if He hated the human body and desired its destruction. It never dawned upon them, however, that these actions were bad and resulted in moral imperfection of the soul. . . . The perfect Torah which leads us to perfection recommends none of these things. On the contrary, it aims at man's following the path of moderation, in accordance with the dictates of nature, eating, drinking, enjoying legitimate sexual relations, all in moderation, and living among people in honesty and uprightness, but not dwelling in the wilderness or afflicting the body."

Healthy living requires also opportunities for aesthetic experience. Gloomy moods will vanish under the spell of music, fine arts, or beautiful sights of nature. "Just as the body becomes exhausted from hard labor and then by rest and refreshment recovers, so it is necessary for the mind to have relaxation by gazing upon pictures and other beautiful objects that its weariness may be dispelled." Even delicacies in food may occasionally be essential. Thus "when one suffers from the loss of appetite, it may be stirred up by highly seasoned delicacies and agreeable, palatable food."[4]

Life is Social

The quest for meeting these objectives makes man a social being. For a single person cannot create the resources on which he depends for his existence.

Man's need for society begins with the quest for a circle of friends. One needs friends for aid and comfort in time of trouble, no less than for the pleasantries of ordinary social intercourse. That need is satisfied in the free relationships of friendship and family life. But man's needs for society carry him beyond the kinship of blood and sentiment. The very necessities of living create an interdependence among all people which forms the basis of an organized social order.

The most important factor making for human interdependence is economic. Citing the various goods and services on which man depends for his bodily life, Maimonides points out: "One man alone cannot procure all this; it is impossible for a single man to obtain this comfort. It is only possible in society."

Social life creates the possibility for a more complex economic enterprise. It facilitates a division of labor among many people in accordance with their differentiated aptitudes under the leadership of a directing executive. This makes for a more efficient process of production, leading to a greater volume and variety of goods. "For the food which man requires for his subsistence demands much work and preparation, which can only be accomplished by reflection and planning, by the utilization of many utensils, and by the employment of numerous individuals, each performing a particular function. That is why they need one person who should guide and unite them, so that their group be properly organized and endure, and that they should cooperate with one another."

The scholar plays an important role in society, but he could not concentrate on his work if other men were not available to do the more prosaic tasks of civilization. As Maimonides put it: "If all men were seekers of wisdom and philosophy, the social order would be destroyed and the human race quickly disappear from the world; because man is very helpless and needs many things. Consequently it would be necessary for him to learn ploughing, reaping, threshing, grinding, baking and how to fashion implements for these tasks, for the purpose of securing his food supply. Similarly he would have to learn spinning and weaving to clothe himself, the building art to provide a shelter, and to fashion tools for all these works. But the life of Methuselah would not be sufficiently long to learn all these occupations which are indispensable to human existence. When in these conditions would he find leisure to study and acquire wisdom? Consequently, there is necessity for other types of men to follow these occupations which are essential in a city, so that the student may have his wants provided, the land may be inhabited and wisdom found among men."

But Maimonides did not favor a social hierarchy in which some were to engage in the pursuits of learning solely and others confine themselves to the mundane affairs of life. He held it a universal human duty to engage in gainful labor. The scholar must not accept a stipend from others. Even the rabbi who carries all the burdens of the active ministry is not to accept remuneration for his services. Like all other men he must strive for economic freedom through some form of gainful occupation. "A man should even suffer the deepest privations rather than have recourse to his fellowmen or throw himself upon the community. Thus the sages exhorted, 'Make thy (living on the) Sabbath as on a week-day, and be not dependent on thy fellow-men.' Even if he be wise and honored, should he grow poor, he must engage in a trade, however lowly, rather than have recourse to charity. 'Flay a carcass in the street and earn a living, and say not, I am a great man and work is below my dignity.' Some of the great sages were hewers of wood, carvers of logs, drawers of water for the gardens, metal workers, smiths; but they asked nothing from the community and refused whatever was offered to them."

The Origin of the State

Human society is not altogether a free association of men; to function effectively it requires organization which brings into being the state. The need for social organization is derived from the wide diversity among people. That diversity is one of the glories of human life, for it is the means by which civilization is enriched with many varied talents. Man is "the highest form in the creation, and he therefore includes the largest number of constituent elements; this is the reason why the human race contains such a great variety of individuals, that we cannot discover two persons exactly alike in any moral quality, or in external appearance."

This diversity unchecked becomes a centrifugal force making for anarchy and social decomposition. To perpetuate itself and to serve the cause of human collaboration to which it is dedicated, society compromises its freedom and transforms itself into an organized, a disciplined state. "The well-being of society demands that there should be a leader able to regulate the actions of man; he must complete every shortcoming, remove every excess, and prescribe for the conduct of all, so that the natural variety should be counter-balanced by the uniformity of legislation and the order of society be well established."

The function of the state is to establish "the best possible relations among men." Its goal is to create a human order in which "we do not do every one as he pleases, desires and is able to do; but every one of us does that which contributes towards the common welfare." Maimonides recognized that many men would not freely abandon the illusions of a self-seeking individualism. The state, therefore, in promoting the common welfare, must have the power to coerce. Such coercion is not tyranny; it is the means of a larger freedom. "If sinners and robbers were not punished, injury would not be prevented at all; and persons scheming evil would not become rarer. They are wrong who suppose that it would be an act of mercy to abandon the laws of compensation for injuries; on the contrary, it would be perfect cruelty and injury to the social state of the country."

The attributes of human nature which constitute the psycho-
logical foundations of the state must be seen as another aspect of
the divine endowment of man, for his perfection as a member of
society. "It being the will of God that our race should exist and
be permanently established, He in His wisdom gave it such properties that man can acquire the capacity of ruling others. Some
persons are therefore inspired with theories of legislation, such as
prophets and law-givers; others possess the power of enforcing the
dictates of the former, and of compelling people to obey them
and to act accordingly." This endowment of man is but another
tribute to the design with which God planned all creation, giving
to each creature the resources essential for its survival.[5]

A Theory of Ethics

Human values thus begin with the quest for self-preservation,
but what larger ends shall we seek after we have achieved that?
All human action is motivated by some ends. But each end in the
usual routine of human interests when carefully examined, proves
but a means to another end; not one of them proves self-sufficient.
Obviously, the chain of ends, or final causes, cannot be an infinite
one; it must commence somewhere with an absolute end, from
which all other goals are derived.

There is only one absolute Being, and that is God. The ultimate purpose of all existence must accordingly be the fulfillment
of whatever is decreed by His will or wisdom, which strictly
speaking is really identical with His essence. In other words, "the
series of the successive purposes terminates . . . in God's will or
wisdom, which in our opinion are identical with His essence and
are not anything separate from Himself or different from His essence." Thus when we carry the drama of existence to its ultimate
meaning we must see it as a quest for God. It may be an unconscious and an inarticulate quest, but it is the one shining light
toward which all the stammerings and stumblings in earthly existence point. The summation of it all is that "God is the final
purpose of everything. . . . It is the aim of everything to become,

according to its faculties, similar to God in perfection. . . . In this sense God is called the end of all ends."

In what way can human conduct endeavor to become "similar to God in perfection"? God's perfection may be gauged, as far as human beings are concerned, by the qualities of His providence as discernible in His government of the universe. Good conduct becomes therefore a striving for the imitation of God, or for the imitation of His providence, as we observe it in nature and in history. This striving for the imitation of God is not imposed on man by external authorities. It is written irresistably in the very texture of his being. And we heed its summons more keenly, as we become God-like and reflect in our own life the very patterns of His providential ordering of the work of existence.

The attributes of divine providence by which we are to model our lives may be summarized, according to Maimonides, in the terms *hesed,* loving-kindness; *zedakah,* righteousness; and *mishpat,* judgment. *Hesed* is pure charity; it is the exercise of kindness to those who have no claim on us or in a measure beyond what they have a claim for. *Zedakah* is a service to others in time of need, inspired not by any formal commitments but by a sense of moral obligation. *Mishpat* is an application of justice and it manifests itself in mercy or punishment. To one who recognizes these virtues as the transcendent qualities of the universe, who can delineate their imprint in the rhythms of cosmic life, and sees them as the distinctive attributes of God's way with His creatures, they become ideals to pattern after, models to emulate.

What we believe about God is thus not unrelated to the moral life. We sometimes assume that the two are totally distinct, because the social consequences of faith in God "become only apparent after a long series of intermediate links, and from a general point of view." In reality, however, faith in God has "results which concern also his fellow-men." When a person has acquired "the knowledge of God, the knowledge of His providence and of the manner in which it influences His creatures in their production and continued existence—he will then be determined always to seek loving-kindness, judgment and righteousness, and thus to imitate the ways of God."

The attributes of divine providence form a pattern of ethics for the state no less than for the individual. The guardians of society must not act arbitrarily toward their citizens; nor should they make statecraft an expression of their private passions or prejudices. They should pattern after the attributes of God's government in the universe. "The governor of a country . . . should conform to these attributes. Acts of government must be performed by him moderately and in accordance with justice, not merely as an outlet for his passions." The state may have to coerce a defiant citizen, judged to be an enemy of the common good, but it must do so without a spirit of hatred. "The governor of a country . . . must be able to condemn a person to death without anger, passion or loathing against him, and must exclusively be guided by what he perceives of the guilt of the person and by a sense of the great benefit which a larger number will derive from such a sentence." The preponderant occupation of government, moreover, must not be the exercise of coercion, but the dissemination of charity and kindness. "Acts of mercy, pardon, pity and grace should more frequently be performed by the governors of a country than acts of punishment."

These same attributes of God's providence also serve as the incentives for a personal morality. An ethically sensitive person, obviously, will not injure another. He will not seek a private advantage through another's hurt. His word will be as sacred as his bond. In all relationships with other human beings his behaviour will be characterized by an uncompromising integrity. Indeed, he will not injure a dumb animal. And he will apply the same code of honor in his dealings with the state as he does in his dealings with individuals. The evasion of taxes, for instance, or another popular evil of that day, the use of a debased coinage, Maimonides denounced as a great moral perversion. "It is forbidden a man to accustom himself to words of flattery or seduction, nor should he be otherwise in his speech than he is in his heart, but alike within as without, so that what is in his heart is identical wth the words in his mouth. Even a single word of seduction or deception is prohibited. Instead, there should be truthful speech, an upright spirit, and a heart pure from treachery and mischief."

A person has a positive obligation to promote the welfare of his fellow man. A callous refusal to aid is the same as to injure; and one who refuses to deliver a person from death though he has the opportunity to do so is as guilty as though he had killed him. "It is not sufficient to give assistance to those who are in need of our help; we must look after their interests, be kind to them, and not hurt their feelings by words." Thus in a business transaction, one must be just as concerned with the interest of the other party as with his own. "Those that are engaged in such transactions must mutually promote each other's interests; neither of the parties must strive to increase only his own profit, and that he alone should enjoy the whole benefit of the transaction."

Touching is the solicitude of Maimonides for the slave. Slavery was an integral part of ancient economic life, but Maimonides sought to safeguard the slave as a personality endowed by the Creator with rights which are sacred. Though the law allows slavery, he wrote, "it is nevertheless of the measure of piety and the way of wisdom to be merciful, to practice justice, not to in-flict a heavy yoke on one's slave, and not to vex him. We ought to give him to eat of every food, and of every drink. The old sages used to give their slaves of every dish they ate themselves, and they fed their cattle and their slaves before they themselves dined. . . . Likewise he must not offend him either with the hand or with words. . . . And thus it says expressly in the beautiful traits of Job which he glorifies in, 'If I did despise the cause of my man-servant, when they contended with me. Did not He that made me in the womb make him?' (Job 31: 13, 15). Hardness of heart is to be found only among the pagan idolators, but the seed of Abraham . . . they are obligated to be merciful over all. And thus it is implied in the attributes of the Holy One, blessed be He, which He commanded us to imitate: 'And his mercies are over all His works' " (Ps. 145:9).

Maimonides was particularly emphatic in urging aid for the underprivileged. "We are in duty bound to be more careful with the fulfillment of the commandment relating to charity than all other commandments. . . . Whoever closes his eyes against charity is called, like the idol-worshipper, impious. . . . Whoever gives alms to the poor with bad grace and downcast looks, though he bestow a thousand gold pieces, all the merit of his action is lost; but he must give with good grace, gladly, sympathizing with the poor man in his trouble. If a poor man solicit alms of you and you have nothing to give him, console him with words; and it is forbidden to upbraid the poor or raise the voice against him since his heart is broken and crushed. . . . Woe, then, to the person who shames the poor man! Be to him rather like a parent, whether in compassion or in kindly word."

Maimonides listed eight degrees of charity, one higher than the other; and these have become well-known. The highest is to aid the poor in regaining self-support by securing for them work or some business opportunity. Where direct giving has to be resorted to, one must be cautious to safeguard the sensibilities of the poor. An arrangement in which the donor and the recipient remain anonymous is ideal. This is to some extent achieved in the community welfare fund, to which however "no contribution should be made without the donor feeling confident that the administration is honest, prudent and capable of management." If this is not available, the giver or the recipient should remain anonymous. It is, of course, better to give before being asked than to wait until one is approached. Giving less than one should is in part redeemed if it is given graciously. The lowest, is giving grudgingly.

A person's moral obligations do not end with members of his own people. A Jew is committed to help non-Jews resident in their midst, to feed their needy, visit their sick or bury their dead and comfort their mourners. God's mercies extend to all His creatures, and ours must be similarly broad and all inclusive.

But the moral law does not only demand loving kindness and righteousness; it also demands judgment, which is the application of justice. And an ethical person must also know when to be stern. Thus, while we must not return a fugitive slave to his master, we must be ready to return a fugitive criminal. A sympathy which is so universal that it refuses to discriminate "between the oppressor and the oppressed" is pure sentimentality and morally an evil. Such "mercy on sinners is cruelty to all creatures."[6]

Maimonides made use of the ethical doctrine of Aristotle that the right action in any situation is a proper balance between two extremes. But this doctrine of the "mean" did not constitute for Maimonides a sufficient theory of ethics. He offered a more cogent anchor for ethical action in his conception of God. He pointed moreover to levels of ethical action which go beyond the principle of balancing extremes. To balance extremes is to seek a frontier marking precisely where lie one's own rights and where commence one's obligations. The truly saintly person, however, will readily yield of himself in uncalculating acts of beneficence for others. He will assume responsibilities for others beyond what is expected of him. He will cheerfully deny himself in service to a greater cause.

The Final Good

Moral growth, however, is not a final good, since it does not exist for its own sake. "For all moral principles concern the relation of man to his neighbor; the perfection of man's moral principles is, as it were, given to man for the benefit of mankind." We can imagine a state where men have mastered to the full the ideal of cooperative living, and we can imagine the individual abstracted from his social milieu. The goals of morality do not apply then. "Imagine a person being alone, and having no connection whatever with any other person, all his good moral principles are at rest; they are not required, and give man no perfection whatever. These principles are only necessary and useful when man comes in contact with the others."

The moral perfection of man is in a sense the social consequence of his closeness to God. But the experience of closeness to

God itself, without reference to the fruits it yields in guiding human relations, is the supreme good of human existence. Maimonides describes this experience as the intellectual worship of God. It is the highest end toward which men must strive throughout their lives on earth.

Maimonides tells a parable to illustrate the varied pathways by which men seek to approach God. The paths vary and so do the results. "I will begin the subject of this chapter," Maimonides explains, "with a simile. A king is in his palace and all his subjects are partly in the country and partly abroad. Of the former, some have their backs turned toward the king's palace, and their faces in another direction; and some are desirous and zealous to go to the palace, seeking 'to inquire in his temple,' and to minister before him, but have not yet seen even the wall of the house. Of those that desire to go to the palace, some reach it, and go round about in search of the entrance gate; others have passed through the gate, and walk about in the ante-chamber; and others have succeeded in entering into the inner part of the palace. But even the latter do not immediately on entering the palace see the king, or speak to him, for, after having entered the inner part of the palace, another effort is required before they can stand before the king . . . at a distance, or close-by . . . hear his words, or speak to him.

"I will now explain the simile which I have made. The people who are abroad are all those that have no religion, neither one based on speculation nor one received by tradition. . . . Those who are in the country, but have their backs turned toward the palace, are those who possess religious belief and thought, but happen to hold false doctrines, which they either adopted in consequence of great mistakes made in their own speculations, or received from others who misled them. Because of these doctrines they recede more and more from the palace the more they seem to proceed. . . . Those who desire to arrive at the palace, and to enter it, but have never yet seen it, are the mass of religious people; the multitude that observe the divine commandments, but are ignorant.

Those who arrive at the palace, but go round about it, are those
who devote themselves exclusively to the study of practical law;
they believe traditionally in the true principles of faith, and learn
the practical worship of God, but are not trained in philosophical
treatment of the principles of the law, and do not endeavor to establish the truths of their faith by proof. Those who undertake to
investigate the principles of religion, have come to the ante-chamber; and there is no doubt that these can also be divided into
different grades. But those who have succeeded in finding a proof
for everything that can be proved, who have a true knowledge of
God, so far as a true knowledge can be attained, and are near
the truth, wherever an approach to the truth is possible, they have
reached the goal, and are in the palace in which the king lives."

The ritual of formal religious devotions is only an aid in the
process of true worship. It serves to withdraw our thoughts from
worldly matters and focus them upon God. And its efficacy is dependent upon the concentration with which it is enacted; the me-
chanical performance of ritual is devoid of significance. "We must
bear in mind that all such religious acts as reading the Torah,
praying and the performance of other precepts, serve exclusively
as the means of causing us to occupy and fill our mind with the
precepts of God and free it from worldly business; for we are thus
as it were in communion with God and undisturbed by any other
thing. If we, however, pray with the motion of our lips . . . but
at the same time think of our business . . . we are like those who
are engaged in digging the ground or hewing wood in the forest,
without reflecting on the nature of those acts, or by whom they are
commanded, or what is their object. We must not imagine that in
this way we attain the highest perfection . . ."

True worship is man's supreme bliss, and he must seek it always.
"You must know that even if you were the wisest man in respect
to the true knowledge of God, you break the bond between you
and God whenever you turn your thoughts entirely to the necessary food and necessary business." One should therefore discipline
himself to maintain his contemplation of God even when attending

to worldly matters. "When you are alone by yourself, when you are awake on your couch, be careful to meditate in such precious moments on nothing but the intellectual worship of God. . . . When we have acquired a true knowledge of God, and rejoice in that knowledge in such a manner, that whilst speaking with others, or attending to our bodily wants, our mind is all that time with God; when we are with our heart constantly near God, even whilst our body is in the society of men; when we are in that state which the song on the relations between God and man poetically describes in the following words (Song of Songs 5:2): 'I sleep but my heart waketh; it is the voice of my beloved that knocketh', —then we have attained not only the height of ordinary prophets, but of Moses, our Teacher . . ."[7]

Chapter VI

THE LEGACY OF MAIMONIDES

The writings of Maimonides have excited the admiration of posterity for their versatility, their erudition and above all for their originality in charting new paths for the human spirit in its effort to know life and to live it nobly. But can Maimonides still guide us in the religious perplexities of our own time? Is the world outlook of Maimonides only an imposing chapter in the history of ideas, or can it contribute insights that will help man in the contemporary dilemmas which confront him in his spiritual life?

Every thinker is to some extent a child of his own time. In his very endeavor to address his thought to his contemporaries, he must take on their own idiom; he must master their universe of discourse and make it his own. Even if his thought embody permanent truth, it will, nevertheless be set in a particular cultural milieu, and take on its specific forms, thus becoming limited by its particular limitations. The permanent and the transient will comingle. The task of posterity will then be to delineate the two, identifying the core of permanent truth and holding on to it as the legacy of the past, while dismissing all else as obsolete.

There is an element in the teachings of Maimonides which is clearly obsolete. It is the medieval conception of the universe which he shared with others of his age and which was an inheritance from Greek thought, especially Aristotle.

Thus Maimonides described the corporeal world as constituted of matter and form; matter he resolved into the ultimate elements of fire, air, water and earth, the proportions into which these elements combine determining the character of specific objects. The total universe, he described, as consisting of three strata. The first strata, the "Intelligences" which are forms without matter, act upon the world of matter to shape its destiny; the second strata, the realm of corporeal beings, constitutes a solid globe containing nine spheres, one within the other, and like the Intelligences, they are not destructible; the third strata consists of transient things such as the bodies of men, plants, animals, and minerals. The ruling power in creation, as he phrased it, "emanates from the Creator and is received by the Intelligences according to their order; from the Intelligences part of the good and the light bestowed upon them is communicated to the spheres, and the latter being in possession of the abundance obtained of the Intelligences, transmit forces and properties unto the beings of this transient world."[1]

The essential concern of Maimonides was however not to perpetuate the Aristotelian cosmology. Indeed, he was aware of its limitations, that it was compounded of "assertions which cannot be proved."[2] He accepted it because it was his conviction that science is an essential stepping stone to religion, that the knowledge of the physical universe was an essential preliminary to the discovery of God's grandeur and beneficence as Creator, and to the experience of awe and love which is the true worship of God. Where else was Maimonides to seek the knowledge of the physical universe than in the science of his time? Aristotelian science was the best his age knew; and he mastered it and drew upon it as an aid in the larger quest, the quest for communion with God.

Maimonides was explicit in reminding his readers that while he employed current scientific knowledge, he was not primarily concerned with propagating it. His primary concern was with the defense of his religious tradition, with charting a way for educated men to continue to find in the faith of their fathers the resources of doctrine and life which they needed for their careers on earth. As Maimonides put it: "It was not my intention when writing this treatise to expound natural science or discuss metaphysical systems . . . for the books written on these subjects serve their purpose, and if in some points they are not satisfactory, I do not think that what I could say would be better than what has been explained by others. Where you therefore notice that I prove the existence and number of Intelligences or the number of the spheres, with the cause of their motion, or discuss the true relation of matter and form, the meaning of Divine manifestations, or similar subjects, you must not think that I intend merely to establish a certain philosophical proposition.. . . . I only desire to mention what might, when well understood, serve as a means of removing some of the doubts concerning anything taught in Scripture."[3]

The true significance of the work of Maimonides was not in his utilization of current scientific knowledge, but in his criticism of the philosophic generalizations that some thinkers drew from it. It was Aristotle's legacy in metaphysics rather than in science which constituted the boldest aspect of Aristotelian thought. For Aristotelian thought did not content itself to remain a description of the process discernible in nature. It attempted to go beyond that and to extend its categories into ultimate interpretations of life in the universe. It generalized its method into a philosophy of naturalism, in which the laws of natural causality are the sole factor in the making of events. In this doctrine, there is no design working itself out in the universe, but only blind necessity; the individual's life is moved by chance, and is not under any special providence of God; there is only one way to truth, and that is reason; and God is only a link in an endless chain of causation which has gone on eternally and which grinds out life and death with complete indifference to human hopes.

It was this phase of Aristotelian thought which constituted the bold challenge to religion, and it was this which Maimonides attacked with uncompromising logic. By what evidence, he asked, did the Aristotelians assert that the universe is eternal, and that there is no more in the life process than natural necessity? There was no evidence. Their assertion was built on an unproven hypothesis. By the canons of evidence, it would be just as plausible to assert the creation of the universe in time. Indeed, it would be more plausible. For the universe we live in does not reveal itself to us as a completely ordered and uniformly working mechanism. It reveals vast realms of freedom too, leaps from one realm of being to another, which cannot be accounted for by the workings of natural necessity. What, for instance, can account for the positions of the stars and the directions of their motions? What can account for the transition from a realm of immaterial "forms" to the realm of concrete material beings? Science can observe and describe what already exists. It is an invaluable chart for our knowledge of the sublunary world. But when we leave the sublunary world, we enter an arena where freedom is discernible, where action tends to suggest the workings of an intelligent and beneficent first cause, but a cause that is free to will and to choose and to initiate without constraint.

Considering the stakes for human life in our choice between these alternatives, Maimonides summoned men to reject naturalism, in favor of the theory of creation. For naturalism would undermine the sources of a sound moral order. It would hurt human morality and human morale. Life would be a process of blind conformity to impersonal laws of natural necessity. Where then would we find an incentive for human initiative to make life more noble? Where would we find an anchor for our moral motivations, for our quest to create freedom and justice in the world? Whence would we get the assurances that our lives are significant and are not doomed to ultimate frustration? Naturalism may have its attraction for a metaphysician, but it is sterile as an outlook on which man is to build his life in the world.

Thus Maimonides was led to reaffirm the conception of God as enunciated in traditional religion, at least an enunciated in the noblest expressions of traditional religion. God, as Maimonides portrayed Him, is Absolute Being; He is not a magnified person. But He is the Creator of the universe, in which He is realizing designs and purposes freely willed by Him; He is above the necessities of nature, which are only His instruments in the unfolding processes of creation; He is the source of order and uniformity in the universe, but He is not bound by it; He can inject Himself into the flow of events to produce miracles, to illumine the prophets, to bestow prophetic leadership upon particular individuals or a particular community and to exercise His providence over individual human beings.[4]

The Maimonidean critique of naturalism should be of more than historical interest to us. For is not the cultural dilemma of our time essentially similar to the one which faced Maimonides? The science of our day is vastly different from the "science" of the medieval world. But the issue which challenges contemporary religion is not science as such, but the generalizations which some men draw from it. And those generalizations are essentially the same basic assumptions of naturalism. Our popular interpretations of life tend to recognize but two factors in history, man and nature, and between the two is enacted the entire drama of man's career on earth. "The historian of today," Eric Frank observed recently, "has recourse to natural factors alone. Man has returned to the ancient Greek idea, according to which history was merely a natural process." Indeed, the sweep of naturalism has gone so far as to bring the phenomenon of religion itself within the scope of its interpretation of existence. "Even religion itself and its concepts of man and his destiny," Frank continues, "have come to be regarded as merely historical phenomena. These concepts are now understood as historically conditioned expressions of certain primitive forms of human thought which gradually had to yield to the more enlightened insight of later generations."[5] Contemporary naturalism differs from its Aristotelian antecedent principally in the rejection of even the vocabulary of traditional religion. The contemporary fashion of thought looks upon the universe as a self-sufficient enterprise, which requires no transcendent source to account for its being or to endow it with significance. It finds no need to employ even the term God.

In this cultural distortion man denies what is due God, but he also robs himself. For he has rejected a great and mighty friendship. Placed in the mansion of the universe which is his home, man has often been unable to understand its mysteries and to formulate the necessary rules of conduct by which he must live in it, thereby running into difficulty. So long as he felt assured that he was placed there by a Friend, he has been confident that he would eventually discover the clue to his happiness. Thus he is ever summoned to try again to continue his labors for the kind of world order which will give him peace. He has in any case the joyous sense of a great friendship, that there is someone who cares for him, to whom he may come with his problem, who will help him through his difficulty.

Far different is the fate of the man who must face the world alone. False bravado prompts a Bertrand Russell to summon man,, to "cherish . . . the lofty thoughts that ennoble his little day," after he has taught that "on him and all his race the slow, sure doom falls pitiless and dark."[6] Faith for living must be built of sterner stuff. It is significant that modern man with all his technical advances stands frightened at his fate. The commodity he seeks most is peace of mind. The most prevalent disease afflicting him is neuroticism. The tallest building in New York City requires a special corps of detectives to keep people from committing suicide by jumping from its summit. We suffer from the inevitable consequences of a secularization of culture, fear of living.

The secularization of culture has lowered human morale and wrought havoc with morality. A secular culture is anthropocentric in the grossest sense. By eliminating God as the center of existence, it leaves man alone to dominate the scene, with his empirical plans and purposes as the sole arbiter of life. He becomes the measure of all things and relates all values to his individual needs. The "moralities" fashioned on secular foundations have proved a weak barrier against brutality and hurt. Individualism, the earliest of these secular moralities, teaches that every man has duties only to himself. In the free competition of individuals, the fittest survive; and only the fittest in such combat need survive. Radical individualism fosters anarchy, leading to reactions which have produced other secular moralities: fascism, racialism, Marxism. The good is here defined as the interests of the national or racial community, or of a particular social class. A tribal morality is thus established, and woe unto those who stand outside the favored tribe!

There have been attempts to formulate a universal morality on a secular basis, the most serious being religious humanism and ethical culture. But when the pursuit of a good conflicts with our own interests, one needs compelling incentives still to cling to the good in spite of the consequences. The religious foundation for such incentives is the doctrine that God, in having fashioned life, has thus showered His love upon it; and that love endows all existence with an intrinsic value. Our conduct must ever be the quest to imitate God's ways in the world. This is how Maimonides motivated ethical action. As W. E. Hocking put it: "No injunction to 'love your neighbor' is obeyable unless your neighbor is in fact lovable. . . . Sociology is completely helpless to give support to the kind of doctrine we need, that man has worth in himself. For sociology knows nothing about values, except by way of human valuations. If somebody actually likes a man, the man may be deemed as having value because of that liking; then if we cease liking him, his value vanishes."[7]

What is the answer to all this? Maimonides would have asked for a re-examination of fundamentals. Can we by reason alone comprehend the universe about us? Is the universe such as our scientific conceptions portray it, an impersonal, eternal enterprise knowing no more than the necessities of nature and being wholly bound by those necessities? In such a universe even God would be a helpless participant in a process over which He exercised no initiative, a process that was endlessly repeating itself without seeking any wise or beneficent end. But there is no evidence to support such a view of the universe.

Naturalism is a hypothesis. It is an exaggeration of the method competent in the inquiries of science into a philosophy of the universe. Reason is precious but it is insufficient in itself to guide life. There is another source of truth, revelation, out of which has come the decisive word about God and the universe, and about the meaning of the drama of human existence on earth. Let reason unite her strength with that of the truth which comes from revelation and as loyal allies let them both labor for the enlightenment of man. Then will man rise to his noblest destiny.

Time as well as thought separate us from the world of Moses

Maimonides. But there is in his thought a kernel of abiding truth. It is the chief glory of his many far-reaching contributions to the Judaism of the ages. It is the principal legacy which his writings have to offer to posterity. When men will seek a view of the universe which will not rob life of its dignity or its hope, they will walk in the footsteps of Moses Maimonides.

NOTES

Chapter I

MOSES MAIMONIDES — HIS LIFE AND WORK

[1] *Kobetz teshubot ha-Rambam,* Leipzig 1859, II p. 28b and cf. A. Marx, "Texts by and about Maimonides," *Jewish Quarterly Review,* N. S. XXV4, pp. 374-381.

[2] D. H. Baneth, *Igrot ha-Rambam,* Jerusalem, 1946, p. 93.

[3] Maimonides finished the *Guide* about 1197, but its final revision was not completed till 1200. See A. Marx, *ibid,* pp. 385-387.

[4] For the discussion of the writings of Maimonides, see Leon Roth, *The Guide for the Perplexed,* London 1948, pp. 20-35. The computation of the commandments in the Mishneh Torah is in the introduction to that work.

[5] The commentary on Rosh Hashanah was published by J. Bruel, in *Yen Lebanon,* Paris 1866, pp. 1-21, and the commentary on Shabbat was published by S. Asaf, in *Sinai* (Hebrew), III 8-9, Jerusalem 1940, pp. 103-132.

[6] For a discussion of the medical writings of Maimonides, see H. Friedenwald, *The Jews and Medicine,* Baltimore 1944, pp. 193-216 and Max Meyerhof, "The Medical Works of Maimonides," in *Essays on Maimonides,* N. Y. 1941, pp. 265-295.

[7] Waldemar Schweisheimer, "Maimonides' Medical Opinions in the Light of Modern Science," *Medical Leaves* V 1943, pp. 80 f.

[8] In *History of Medicine,* London 1910, I p. 374, quoted by H. Friedenwald, *ibid,* p. 216.

[9] D. H. Baneth, *ibid,* pp. 31-85, 91-94, 95-96.

Chapter II

REASON AND THE QUEST FOR TRUTH

[1] Moreh I 5, 17, II 21, 23, 26, III 17, 21; Letter to the Jews of Marseilles (Hebrew), *Kobetz Teshubot ha-Rambam ve-Igrotov,* ed. Leipzig 1859, II p. 25b, and *ibid,* Letter to R. Hisdai ha-Levi, p. 23a, Letter to R. Judah ibn Tibbon, p. 28b, Essay on the Resurrection, p. 9a, Essay against Galen, pp. 20b, 21b. Maimonides frequently refers to his adversaries by the general name "philosophers." By this he had in mind those who endeavor to interpret existence by means of reason alone, without reference to Scripture. The designation thus covered all the representatives of Greek thought, and their later disciples. In most cases, however, Maimonides deals specifically with the challenge of Aristotelian thought, because Aristotle was the most important figure among the philosophers. Maimonides was clearly aware of the writings of other Greek thinkers, apart from Aristotle. Thus he spoke of various schools of philosophy, including those who preceded Plato and he of course, regarded Plato as one of the very important philosophers (in letters to R. Judah ibn Tibbon and R. Hisdai ha-Levi). In the Essay on Resurrection he refuses to recognize the Mutakallemim as philosophers because they did not pursue rigorous analysis in their studies. In the Letter to the Jews of Yemen, ibid, p. 1b, he cites the writings of various pagan thinkers among them the Greeks, as adversaries of the Torah. Cf. Leo Strauss, "The Literary Character of the Guide," in Essays on Maimonides, ed. by S. Baron, N. Y. 1941, pp. 41f.

[2] *Moreh,* I 71.

[3] *Moreh,* Introduction.

[4] *Moreh,* I 1, 72, 73; III 8; Commentary on Mishnah, Introduction; Eight Chapters, ch. 1, 2; *Millot ha-Higayon* section 9, 10.

[5] Commentary on Mishnah, Introduction; *Moreh,* I 34.

[6] *Moreh,* III, 51, 54; *Yad,* Yesode ha-Torah 2: 1, 2, 4:12, Teshubah, 4:12, 10:3, 10:6; *Sefer ha-Mitzvot,* Positive commandment, 3, Kobetz, p. 28b. The awe felt before God's greatness is here taken as a fulfillment of the duty to "fear the Lord thy God" (Deut. 10:20). However, in *Sefer ha-Mitzvot,* Positive Commandment 4, Maimonides applies this verse to the fear deriving from the prospect of God's punishment. The divergence becomes clear when we consider the character of the *Sefer ha-Mitzvot.* As Maimonides makes clear in the introduction, this treatise was intended to defend his computation of the commandments as employed in the *Yad,* against the anticipated objections of the common people who had been habituated to follow the system of computations formulated by Rabbi Simon Kahira in his *Halakot*

Gedolot. The common people, of course, were incapable of reaching the fear of God at its highest level. It was a common doctrine of Maimonides that the prescriptions of the Torah addressed themselves to the common people, at their level of understanding, while for the educated the same texts, in a more figurative rendition, conveyed a deeper meaning. The fact that the *Sefer ha-Mitzvot* was intended for the common people may explain certain other differences in the treatment of the same material between this work and other writings of Maimonides. Cf. B. Z. Bokser, "Sefer ha-Mitzvot u-Mishneh Torah" (Hebrew), in *Bitzaron,* Heshvan 5709, pp. 85-96. On the two levels of the fear of God cf. Albo, *Ikkarim,* III 33 and Rabenu Behay, *Hobot ha-Lebabot* III 3, where the distinction is explicitly made, with the lower level of fear corresponding to the capacities of the uneducated. The lower level of fear is of course seen as provisional, to be superseded by the higher fear, as intellectual development progresses. Maimonides denied that the Torah is eternal, as was taught for example in Philo's doctrine of the *logos.* The Torah was for him a creation in time, like any part of nature. He often called attention to many striking parallels between the Torah and nature (*Moreh* I 65, III 32, 34). It is thus understandable that the study of the commandments would serve even as the study of nature to reveal the greatness of God.

⁷ *Moreh,* I 31-36, 72; II 23; Letter to R. Hisdai ha-Levi, 23a. The distrust for the intellectual competence of youth appears in Plato, *Republic* VII where he objects to young men studying dialectics. The power of habit as a hindrance in the pursuits of reason is described by Maimonides as new, while the other difficulties were already recognized by Alexander of Aphrodisias. Leo Strauss, *Philosophie und Gesetz,* Berlin 1935, p. 46, has made the plausible suggestion that Maimonides is referring especially to the habituated interpretations of Scripture, which he indeed mentions to illustrate his general point. The Greeks did not have an authoritative Scripture, whose conventional interpretations could have impeded their speculations.

⁸ *Moreh,* III 17, II 13-29, Essay against Galen, pp. 22a, 22b, Essay on the Resurrection, pp. 10b, 11a, Letters to Marseilles Jewry and to R. Hisdai ha-Levi, pp. 23a, 23b, 24a, 25b, 26a.

⁹ *Moreh* I 2, II 40, III 27, 33, 35; *Yad,* Melakim 7:1, 9:1; *Commentary on Mishnah,* Eight Chapters, ch. 6; *Millot ha-Higayon, section* 8:14; Aristotle, *Nichomachean Ethics,* I 1, 7, II 2, VI 5, 7, VII 1. Cf. D. Rosin, *Die Ethik des Maimonides,* Breslau 1876, pp. 36f, 81f. Maimonides rejects explicitly the view, maintained by Saadia and others, that there is a category of "rational" laws which we could deduce by reason, even if they were not ordained in Scripture. There are laws on which there is a general consensus among men. Maimonides calls those laws *Meforsumos,* "widely established laws." But they have no essential anchor in reason. This may be why Maimonides insists that adherents of the seven Noahite laws, to qualify as "pious men among the gentiles" must accept those laws as Scripturally ordained, rather than as universal rational imperatives. It is significant too that Maimonides lists the prohibitions of incest and unchastity, two Nohahic commandments, among the revealed rather than among the so-called rational

laws. See Commentary on Mishnah, Eight Chapters, ch. 6; *Yad*, Melakim 8:11, 9:1. Maimonides did not consider the question of "natural law" in the field of morals. It is obvious, however, that he must have denied a natural law rooted in the dictates of reason, since the content of the natural law is the same as that of the rational laws. Aristotle speaks of natural law, but Maimonides seems to have regarded this law as "natural" only in a metaphorical sense, as did Averroes and Marsilius of Padua. See Leo Strauss "The Law of Reason in the Kuzari," *Proceedings* of the American Academy for Jewish Research, XIII, 1943, pp. 47-50 and n. 5. Hugo Grotius ascribed a doctrine of natural law to Maimonides, on the basis of *Moreh* III 26. But Grotius misinterpreted Maimonides, as was shown by I. Husik, "The Law of Nature, Hugo Grotius and the Bible," *Hebrew Union College Annual* II 1925, p. 399 n. 10. See also L. Strauss, *ibid*, p. 48 n. 4.

Chapter III

HOW SHALL WE THINK OF GOD?

[1] *Yad,* Yesode ha-Torah 1:1-8; Commentary on Mishnah, Introduction to Helek; Moreh I 71, 72, II Introduction 1, 2, 12, 13, III 17; Responsum to R. Hisdai ha-Levi, in *Kobetz* 23a-b; Letter to Jews of Marseilles, *ibid,* 25b. According to the fourth and fifth propositions in *Moreh* II Introduction, the term motion is applied "in a general sense to all kinds of change, including every transition from potentiality to actuality."

[2] *Moreh* I 36.

[3] *Moreh* I 51, 52, 55-60, III 20. Cf. H. A. Wolfson, "Maimonides on Negative Attributes," in Louis Ginzberg *Jubilee Volume,* pp. 411-446.

[4] *Moreh* II 12-29, III 13; Commentary on Mishnah, Eight Chapters ch. 8; Letter to R. Hisdai ha-Levi and Marseilles Jewry. In *Moreh* III 13 Maimonides appears to infer creation from Aristotle's views concerning the teleology of all things within the sublunary world, which is strange, since he generally holds that events within the sublunary world may be explained satisfactorily in terms of the workings of natural causality. Maimonides apparently presupposes here the previously established argument concerning the character of the spheres, and their motions. Since these deviate from the workings of teleology, showing no useful purpose and eluding all explanations in terms of natural causality, we must assume creation. See H. A. Wolfson, "Halevi and Maimonides on Design, Chance, and Necessity," in *Proceedings,* American Academy for Jewish Research, XI 1941, p. 154. Dr. Wolfson has traced the theory concerning a volitional emanation proceeding eternally, to Ibn Gabirol, *Fons Vitae* I, 7. See H. A. Wolfson, "The Problem of the Origin of Matter in Medieval Jewish Philosophy and its Analogy to the Modern Problem of the Origin of Life," in *Proceedings,* Sixth International Congress of Philosophy, 1926, p. 604.

[5] *Moreh* I 73-76; III 17, II 13-29; Essay against Galen 22a, 22b, Essay on the Resurrection 10b, 11a, Letters to Marseilles Jewry and to R. Hisdai ha-Levi 23a, 23b, 24a, 25b, 26a. "Natural law" is not a very common term in medieval philosophy. According to the common medieval view all substances are endowed with fixed properties from which flow certain types of activity, and they flow necessarily because of the properties inherent in the essence of those substances, or because of their natures. Maimonides believed in this doctrine of nature, but since God is the creator of nature, He may respect those necessities but is not wholly bound by them. From the standpoint of Maimonides the Aristotelian system would negate the supernatural. In Aristotle the term natural is confined to what is constituted of matter and form, so that anything immaterial is above nature. From the standpoint of Mai-

monides the supernatural is the realm of God's free activity which transcends the realm of necessity. Cf. E. Gilson, *The Spirit of Medieval Philosophy*, N. Y. 1936, pp. 365, 472 f, n. 8. Maimonides was aware of the interpretation of the rabbis according to which "miracles are to some extent also natural; for they say when God created the universe with its present physical properties, He made it part of these properties, that they should produce certain miracles at certain times." It is significant that Maimonides calls this interpretation "strange," and that after the statement of his own position he adds: "This should be our belief." See *Moreh* II 29. Why did not Maimonides accept the views of the rabbis which would have brought him into closer harmony with the philosophers? And why does he find that view "strange?" Clearly he wanted a more explicit repudiation of the Aristotelian doctrine of determinism, in which God Himself is bound by the laws of cause and effect. Cf. Moreh II 25 where he rejects the allegorization of miracles as proposed by certain Moslem theologians identified by S. Munk, *Le Guide des Egares*, Paris, 1861, II p. 197 and n. 2 as the Batenis. In a created universe where God can act freely, miracles are possible. Nevertheless, because the universe normally acts in accordance with the nature of things, the burden is always upon us to seek a natural interpretation for events, including those recorded in Scripture, "for it is well known that we are very eager to avoid notions involving an alteration in the order of creation" (Essay on Resurrection). Cf. Commentary on Mishnah, Eight Chapters, ch. 8, where he quotes the rabbinic interpretation of miracles including them in natural law, with no allusion to his dissent.

[6] *Moreh* II 6, 7.

[7] *Moreh* I 58, 70, 72 II 24, 25, III 17, 13, 25.

Chapter IV

RELIGION IN CULTURE

[1] *Moreh* II 4.

[2] *Moreh* I 10, 76 (2), II 44, 45; *Yad,* Yesode-ha Torah 7:2, 3. The divine light is used synonymously with the Shekinah and the Glory of God. Cf. H. A. Wolfson, "Halevi and Maimonides on Prophecy." *JQR, N. S.* XXXIII I, p. 77.

[3] *Moreh* I 65, II 12, 33, 36, 44; Commentary on Mishnah, Introd. to Helek. In *Moreh* II 44, Maimonides suggests that the voices heard by the prophet were part of the prophetic vision which had only a subjective existence; they were "created in the imagination" of the prophet, as the commentators (Shem Tob and Efodi) put it. However, it would be difficult to explain the voices heard by Moses on that basis, since he prophesied without the use of the imaginative faculty. In *Moreh* I 65 and II 33, he discusses the voice heard by Moses and treats it as though it had objective existence. Presumably "the created voice" would then be a miracle. In his letter to R. Hisdai ha-Levi he admits that he would have preferred interpreting the hearing of voices by Moses as a metaphor for the process of contemplation, but the explicit declaration in Scripture made such interpretation far fetched: "As for the sound heard by Moses, undoubtedly it was a created sound formed in nature. But many have said that there was no speech, body or sound in the process, except that the soul of Moses had become absorbed in the contemplation of exalted intellectual concepts, and he comprehended and heard by means of true discourse, which is the contemplation of divine doctrines. . . . Were it not that Scripture repeatedly states (Nu. 7:89): 'And he heard the voice speaking to him,' I would accept the latter interpretation." Cf. Z. Diesendruck, "Maimonides' Lehrs von der Prophetie," in *Jewish Studies in Memory of Israel Abrahams,* N. Y. 1927, pp. 124-132.

[4] *Moreh,* Introduction, I 46, 73, II 32, 36, 37, 38: *Yad,* Yesode ha-Torah 7:4, 5, 6, 7, 10:3; Commentary on Mishnah, Eight Chapters, ch. 7; *Sefer-ha-Mitzvot,* Negative Commandments, 31; Letter to Yemenite Jews, 6b. For the role of the imagination in prophecy, see Leo Strauss, *ibid,* pp. 91-108. Maimonides contrasts his doctrine of prophecy with the vulgar view of the "fools," among whom he includes spokesmen of popular religion among his own people and with the views of the philosophers. The vulgar view makes prophecy entirely a matter of God's free grace; training and preparation are not essential pre-requisites. For the philosophers, on the other hand, prophecy is a necessary result of certain perfections to which the prophet has attained. These views on prophecy, Maimonides adds, all

derive from the position taken by those respective thinkers on the origin of the universe. Maimonides does not clarify this relationship fully, but it becomes clear when we realize that the divisions on prophecy are in truth divisions on the manner in which events are produced. The philosophers, by whom Maimonides obviously understands the Aristotelians, teach the eternity of the universe, and as a consequence, hold the realm of natural causality as absolute. All events in nature transpire in inescapable conformity to the laws of cause and effect, and even God Himself cannot alter the necessities of nature. Prophecy would therefore likewise have to follow this general law of causation and it would have to be a result of a perfection in the prophet. By the "fools" Maimonides probably meant especially the Mutakallemim and their disciples who had denied all natural necessity. All events were for them direct interventions of God, who acts in complete freedom without reference to any properties inherent in the nature of things. Prophecy would therefore likewise derive wholly from the choice of God, and the quality of the prophet's life would have no bearing on the matter. Maimonides believed in a realm of natural causality, but this was not absolute. There was still a realm of freedom within which God could act temporarily to suspend the operation of natural causality, as is illustrated in miracles. In its normal functioning, therefore, prophecy follows the requirements of any natural process, and pre-supposes due preparation from the prophet. But God may still intervene temporarily to withhold prophecy from a person duly qualified for it. Cf. I. Abarbanel, on *Moreh* II 32 and Z. Diesendruck, *ibid,* p. 78. Arab philosophers had a special reason for relaxing in the requirements of intellectual perfection as a condition for prophecy in order to account for the prophetic gifts of Mohammed. Cf. H. A. Wolfson, *ibid,* p. 72, n. 182.

⁵ *Moreh* II 35, III 8; II 39, *Yad,* Yesode ha-Torah 7:6, 9:1; Commentary on Mishnah, Helek, 7; Hullin 7:7; Responsum to Joseph ben Gabar of Baghdad, Kobetz II, 15b, 16a, Letter to Yemenite Jews, 4a, Letter to Joseph b. Judah, 30b; Cf. M. Joel *Die Religionsphilosophie des Moses ben Maimon,* Breslau 1859, pp. 30f. In his Letter to Yemenite Jews, 4a, he affirms explicitly that "we believe a prophet or we reject him only on the ground of the nature of his prophecy, and not on the ground of his descent," and he cites Job, Zophar, Bildad, Eliphaz, and Elihu, who were all non-Jews and yet rose to prophecy. But this, according to H. A. Wolfson, *ibid,* pp. 73f, is inconclusive since these men represented one of the lower levels of prophecy, as indicated in *Moreh* II 45. However, elsewhere in the same discussion he seems to include non-Jewish prophets in the same class as Isaiah and Jeremiah. Similarly, in *Yad,* Yesode ha-Torah 9:I, he appears to discuss the characteristics of the genuine prophets, and he mentions the possibility of there being non-Jews among them. Such non-Jewish prophets would of course have to be adherents of the seven Noahite commandments. If they observed the Torah in full they would no longer be non-Jews. On the other hand they could not be teachers of a new religion since any true prophet must conform to the teachings of Moses.

⁶ *Yad,* Introduction, Yesode ha-Torah 9:1-4, Mamrim 1, 2; *Sefer ha*

Mitzvot, Principles 1-3; Commentary on Mishnah, Introduction. The prophet as prophet was not authorized to promulgate independent enactments or to interpret the law. The Talmud ascribed many new enactments to various prophets but in the institution of those enactments the prophets acted in conjunction with their "courts" as was the case with rabbinic authorities. On all matters subject to deliberation, the prophet's authority was no greater than that of any scholar. In an emergency, however, the distinctive leadership functions of the prophet come into play and he could act alone.

[7] *Moreh,* II 33, *Yad,* Yesode ha-Torah 8:1, 2, 3; Letter to Jews of Yemen, 2b, 3a, 4a. On the basis of textproofs from Scripture and from rabbinic writings, Maimonides held that in the case of the first two commandments the people heard the sound but did not comprehend it. In the case of the following eight commandments they did not even hear the sound. But Crescas in his commentary, *Moreh, ad locum,* rejects the view of Maimonides as untenable, and insists that the people heard all the ten commandments. Halevi who did not require intellectual perfection for prophecy saw no difficulty in the notion that all the people heard all the ten commandments. Cf. H. A. Wolfson, *ibid,* p. 67. The sound heard by the people without comprehension but by Moses with full comprehension was of course the "created" sound, miraculously produced for the occasion, as has been noted above. Significant is the comment of Maimonides at the close of his discussion concerning the Sinaitic revelation: "The truth of that conception and how the matter really transpired is very deeply hidden from us, for there has never been nor will there ever be again anything like it. Note it."

[8] *Moreh* II 40, III 41; *Yad,* Yesode ha-Torah, 9, 10; Commentary on Mishnah, Introduction. Cf. *Moreh* I 65 and II 28.

[9] *Moreh,* Introduction, I 34, 54, 69, II 16, 25, III Introduction, 1-7, 10, 28, 35, 39, 42, 48, 54; *Sefer ha-Mitzvot,* Positive Commandments 4; Commentary on Mishnah, Nedarim 3:6, Kelim 12:7, Introduction to Helek; *Yad,* Teshubah 9:1, 10:1-6, Melakim 10:12, 12:4, Tum'at Oklin 16:12, Abadim 9:8, Mattenot Aniyim 10:1-14, Deot 1:5, 6, 12:6. For the Maimonidean conception of the Torah as the blueprint for the good society, see Leo Strauss, *ibid,* pp. 59-67, 108-122. The rule to help needy non-Jews is Talmudic, but in the Talmud it is to be done "for the sake of peace." Maimonides based it on the universal character of God's mercy.

[10] *Moreh* I 26, 46, 52, 54, 59, 61, II 29, 31, 43, III 24, 35, 43, 44, 45, 50, 57; *Yad,* Yesode ha-Torah 1:9-12. Prayer and the various other religious rites are a means of intellectual perfection in that they teach important religious doctrines. But they may also help those who have attained intellectual perfection to concentrate on God and to avoid the distractions of the world. Thus they are a means to man's highest end, which is communion with God.

[11] *Moreh,* I 34, II 32, 39, III 8, 27, 33, 35, 54; *Teshubot,* ed. H. Freimann, section 370; Cf. B. Cohen, "The Responsum of Maimonides concerning Music," in Jewish Music Journal, II 2; Commentary on Mishnah, Eight Chapters, ch. 4. The Maimonidean doctrine of the Golden Mean was undoubtedly

influenced by Aristotle, but it had ample precedents in Rabbinic writings.
Cf. S. Goldman, "*The Jew and the Universe*" N. Y. 1936, p. 133; D. Rosin,
Die Ethik des Maimonides, Breslau 1876, p. 26, n. 1.

[12] *Moreh* II 37, 40. The Maimonidean conception of morality as a technique for man's physical perfection accounts for his having placed the
discussion of hygiene and medicine in the general section of his code which
deals with morals. See *Yad,* Deot ch. 4.

[13] *Sefer ha-Mitzvot,* Principle 9; *Moreh* III 26, 29, 30, 31, 34, 35, 37, 39,
50; Letter to Hisdai ha-Levi, 23b. This shows the keen appreciation of
Maimonides for the study of history. It has been maintained that Maimonides
deprecated history because in his Commentary on Mishnah Abot, I, end, he
brands as idle talk "the tales of most people on what transpired and what
was and what the customs of that king are in his palace, and how that one
died, or another became wealthy." But this is not history; it is idle gossip
and Maimonides correctly brands it as such. Cf. Commentary on Mishnah,
Eight Chapters, Ch. 5 where he specifically recommends the study of history
where it is presented with a didactic end in view. In *Moreh* III 26 Maimonides admitted that within the general scope of the commandments
which are rational there might be non-rational elements. Thus while we may
find a good reason for animal sacrifice, "we cannot say why one offering
should be a lamb, whilst another is a ram; and why a fixed number of them
should be brought. . . . It is almost similar to the nature of a thing which
can receive different forms, but actually receives one of them. We must not
ask why this form and not another which is likewise possible, because we
should have to ask the same question if instead of its actual form the thing
had any of the other possible forms." In *Moreh* III 34, he likewise admitted
that the utility of the commandments might not appear in exceptional individuals, even as in the case with the utility of the laws of nature; they are
both addressed to the normal man. A universal principle is only imperfectly
realized in particular cases. Cf. Aristotle, *Nicomacheon Ethics,* V. 7.

[14] *Moreh,* Introduction, I 26, 46, 52, 54, 59, 61, II 6, 8, 11, 29, 30,
40, 47, 48; III Introductions, I-8, 25, 41; *Yad,* Yesode ha-Torah 1:9-12;
Commentary on Mishnah, Introduction; Letter to Yemenite Jews, 2a. In
one sense the *Moreh* was thus an attempt to reveal the secrets of the Law,
what Scripture had intended to be veiled from the general public. To avoid
the transgression he composed his work in the form of a letter to an individual, who, being duly prepared for it, was entitled to have the matter
expounded to him. He also employed a method of hints rather than of
explicit statement which would keep his ideas more or less obscure to an
ill-prepared reader who might come upon his work. For this entire subject
cf. Leo Strauss, "The Literary Character of the Guide," pp. 37-91.

[15] *Moreh* I 32, 58, 70, 72, II 24, 25, III 1-7, 12, 13, 25, 28, 51, 52; *Yad,*
Yesode ha-Torah, 2:1-2; Meila 8:8, Akum 2:3; *Sefer ha-Mitzvot,* Positive
Commandments, 3, Negative Commandments, 47, Essay on the Resurrection,
10a. The teleology of creation is evident in the Torah no less than in nature.
In *Sefer ha-Mitzvot* Negative Commandments, 47, Maimonides regards the
pre-occupation with speculations concerning matter beyond the competence

of reason as a violation of Scriptural law. Cf. Abraham ibn Daud, *ha-Emunah ha-Ramah*, Berlin 1919, p. 100. " 'And thou shalt love the Lord Thy God with all thy heart and with all thy soul and with all thy might.' This commandment includes the imperative to investigate, for it is impossible that a person shall love anything with an intense love without knowing it."

16 *Moreh* I 71, II 8; *Yad*, Yesode ha-Torah 7:2, Ishut 1:13, Malveh ve-Loveh 15:2; Letter to Marseilles Jewry, 25a; Commentary on Mishnah, Introd., Erubin 4:1, Gittin 8:1, Cf. L. Finkelscherer, *Moses Maimunis' Stellung zum Aberglauben und zur Mystik*, Breslau, 1894, pp. 45-93.

17 *Moreh*, Introduction, I 26, 46, 71, II 6, 8, 11, III Introduction, 1-7.

18 *Yad*, Teshubah, 3:8, Akum 1:2, 3, Melakim 11:3, 4, 12:4, 5, 8:10, Shemitah ve-Yobel 13:12-13, Maakolot Asurot 11:1, 13:11 Commentary on Mishnah, Abodah Zarah 1:3, Sanhedrin 1:3; Hullin 1:4, Abot ch. 1; *Moreh* I 59, 63, II 36, Teshubot sec. 63, 42, 124, 364, 369, 370; *Sefer ha-Mitzvot*, Positive Commandments 3, 4; Letter to R. Hisdai ha-Levi, Treatise on Resurrection, Letter to Yemenite Jews.

Chapter V

MAN AS A CITIZEN OF THE UNIVERSE

[1] *Moreh,* II 11, III, 12, 13, 14, 25. Cf. M. Duwshany, "Bayat ha-Takhlit ezel ha-Rambam," *Sinai* VI 1-3, pp. 162-176 and Z. Diesendruck, "Die Teleologie bei Maimonides," *Hebrew Union College Annual* V (1928), pp. 415-535. Cf. his introduction to the Mishnah, where Maimonides regards man as the final end of all things in the sublunary world. The position in *Moreh* III 13 apparently represents a revision of his original view.

[2] Commentary, Mishnah, Introduction, Eight Chapters, ch. 4, 8. Cf. Letters to R. Hisdai ha-Levi and to Marseilles Jewry; *Yad,* Deot, 6:1-2, Teshubah 5:1-5, 6:2-5, 7:1-8; *Moreh,* III 20, 21 *Teshubot,* section 345.

[3] *Moreh* I 70, II 27, III 8-24, 51; *Yad,* Yesode ha-Torah 4:8, 9, Teshubah 8:1-8; Commentary on Mishnah, Introduction to Helek; Essay on Resurrection.

[4] *Yad,* Deot 3:1-3; Deot 4:1-23, Commentary on Mishnah, Eight Chapters 1-5; Abot 1:6; *Teshabot,* section 370. However, for most people Maimonides held that the music of the prayers constituted sufficient aesthetic release. The general music in vogue at the time was usually licentious in character and was rendered by female singers, and Maimonides sought to discourage it. Cf. B. Cohen, "The Responsum of Maimonides Concerning Music," in the *Jewish Music Journal,* II 2, Cf. Also *Moreh* III 8, where he decries songs about 'drink and love,' and Max Meyerhof, "The Medical Works of Maimonides," in *Essays on Maimonides,* ed. by S. Baron, N. Y. 1941, p. 283 f, who cites a medical prescription of Maimonides recommending music to ease the melancholy moods of a patient.

[5] *Moreh* I 69, 72; *Moreh* II 40, III 27, 35, 49; Commentary on Mishnah, Introduction; *Yad,* Mattenot Aniyim 10:18, Deot 1:6.

[6] *Moreh* I 54, 69, 72, III 10, 35, 39, 42, 48, end; *Yad,* Abadim 9:8, Mattenot Aniyim 10: 1-14, Melakim 10:12; Commentary on Mishnah, Nedarim 3:6, Kelim 12:7. The rule to help needy non-Jews is Talmudic (Gittin 61a), but in the Talmud it is to be done "for the sake of peace," a consideration of expendiency. Maimonides based it on the universal character of God's mercy.

[7] *Yad,* Yesode ha-Torah 2:1-2, 4:12, 5:4, 11, Deot 1:2, 4, 5, 6, 7, Zizit 3:11; *Moreh* III 51, end.

Chapter VI

THE LEGACY OF MAIMONIDES

[1] Yad, Yesode ha-Torah 2:3, Moreh II 11.

[2] Moreh II 3.

[3] Moreh II 2.

[4] Because Maimonides leaned on the teachings of Aristotle for the explanations of the natural order, it has been asserted by some that Maimonides was an Aristotelian, an adherent of Greek philosophy and that his professions of traditionalism were meant only to appease the orthodox. But he could have chosen alternatives to many of his views, which were consistent with tradition, and which would have brought him closer to Greek thought. Thus he could have followed the Platonic doctrine of the origin of the universe, introducing an eternal matter as the stuff out of which the universe was fashioned. This doctrine, he held reconcilable with the teachings of Scripture, and he called attention to such a view in the Pirke de R. Eliezer (Moreh, II 13, 25, 26). On the question of miracles, he could have followed the Talmudic interpretation which asserts that miracles, instead of interrupting the necessities of nature, had really been included in those necessities at the time of creation. Indeed, he could have explained away miracles altogether by allegorizing their meaning as had been done by a school of Moslem theologians, the *Batenis*. Instead he chose in all those instances a thorough-going repudiation of philosophy in favor of the teachings of tradition.

[5] *Philosophical Understanding and Religious Truth*, New York, 1945, pp. 118, ff.

[6] *A Free Man's Worship*, in *Selected Papers of Bertrand Russell*, N. Y. 1927, p. 14.

[7] *Science and the Idea of God*, Chapel Hill, 1944, pp. 73, 76.

INDEX

INDEX

Abot, 5
Abraham, 12, 46, 64-66, 97
Abrahams, I., VII
Absolute Being, 26
Adam, 67
Aknin, Joseph ibn, 7, 11
animal sacrifices, 54
Al-Afdhal, 2
Alexander of Hales, 8
Allah, 69
Almohades, 2, 68
Al-Razi, 80
Amos, 70
angels, 36, 37, 59, 60, 63
aphorisms, 9
Arabic, 65
Arabs, 87
Aristotle, 7, 10, 13-15, 19, 25, 26, 32, 33, 38, 41, 59, 63, 73, 103, 105, 107; ethical doctrine of, 99
Aristotelian cosmology, 104
Aristotelian psychology, 41
armed forces, 70
asceticism, 89
Ashariya, 34
astral determination, 77
astrology, 62, 72, 77
astronomy, 52
Al-Afdhal, Sultan, 9
atoms, 34
Aquinas, Thomas, 8

Baran, S., VII
beauty, 81
Bereshit Rabbah, 63
Bible, 7, 8, 41, 42, 75
Biblical law, 67
bodily existence, 89
bodily form, 87
body, 88-90; non-existence of, 87
"The Book of Precepts," 7, 10

Cabbalists, 8
causal force, 78
causality, 14, 45
cause and effect, laws of, 51
charity, 95, 98
Christianity, 67, 68
Chronicles, 41
circumcision, 46
Cohen, A., VII
Columbia University Press, VII
commandments, 56, 68, 87
community welfare fund, 98
conduct, moral, code of, 13
convert, 66
corporeal beings, realm of, 104
cosmic creation, 74

cosmic life, 36
creation, 14, 22, 25, 32, 33, 51, 60, 75, 80, 84, 94, 104, 106
creative energies, 65
criminal, 99
cruelty, 81

Daniel, 41
David, 18
Day of Atonement, 75
death, 81, 85
demonology, 62
diaspora, 69, 70
diet, 54, 89
discipline, 22
divine communion, 85
divine element, 86
divine essence, 32
divine influence, 45
divine law, 1, 46
divine manifestations, 105
divine providence, 73
divine revelation, 23, 67

earth, 74
Egypt, 68
environment, 76
Epistle to Yemen, 8
Epstein, I., VII
Essay on the Calendar, 4
Essay on the Resurrection of the Dead, 8
essential attributes, 29, 31
eternal life, 88
eternalists, 33
ethics, theory of, 94-99
evil, 22, 23, 53, 79-83, 85, 87, 93, 99
"evil impulse," 83
exile, 70
existence, 81
Ezekiel, 42, 58, 60, 63

faith, 51, 60
family life, 91
fascism, 108
Finkelstein, Dr. Louis, VIII
first cause, 26, 34
form, 103, 105
Frank, Eric, 107
free will, 72, 76, 79, 84
freedom, 106; human, 76-78
friendship, 91

Gabar, Joseph ibn, 11
Galenism, 9
Genesis, 60, 63
Ginzberg, Dr. Louis, VIII, 8
God, as Absolute Being, 26-28; creative processes of, 38; essence of, 30; ex-